# THE MAN WHO BOUGHT HIMSELF

## The Story of Peter Still

## by Peggy Mann and Vivian W. Siegal

MACMILLAN PUBLISHING CO., INC.
New York
COLLIER MACMILLAN PUBLISHERS
London

We are especially grateful to Joseph Marks for his unflagging encouragement in the preparation of this version of Peter Still's story; to Landis Olesker for his help in uncovering aspects of Southern law in the 1830s; to John Miller, Chief of the American History Division, New York Public Library; to the entire staff of the New York Society Library; to Professor Stanley F. Chyet, Associate Director of the American Jewish Archives in Cincinnati; and to Betty Borger, who was especially helpful in the copy editing of the manuscript.

Macmillan Publishing Co., Inc.
866 Third Avenue, New York, N.Y. 10022

*Map by Rafael Palacios*
Printed in the United States of America
1  2  3  4  5  6  7  8  9  10

Library of Congress Cataloging in Publication Data
Mann, Peggy.    The man who bought himself.    Bibliography: p.
    1. Still, Peter—Juvenile literature. 2. Slavery in the United States—
    Juvenile literature. [1. Still, Peter. 2. Slavery in the United States.
    3. Negroes—Biography] I. Siegal, Vivian W., joint author. II Title.
E444.S849  301.44'93'0924  [B]  [92]  75-15514  ISBN 0-02-762220-7

To David, Nina, and Lewis
—V. S.
And to our editor, Elizabeth Shub

# Author's Note

———————◆———————

In the year 1855 a man named Peter Still narrated his remarkable life story to Kate E. R. Pickard. The following year she published it as a book, *The Kidnapped and the Redeemed*.

*The Man Who Bought Himself* is a retelling of Peter's unique story, based on that book. Much of the dialogue is taken directly from the original book, as spoken by Peter and his wife to Miss Pickard. However, no attempt has been made to reproduce the varied dialects of the pre–Civil War era. To do so would merely interfere with the readability of this book, without adding to its accuracy—for language experts agree that there is no way to assure the validity of written transcriptions of these regional accents.

Some of the events of Peter's life are so improbable that they could never be included in a work of fiction, because they would never be believed. They are related here for a good and simple reason: they happened.

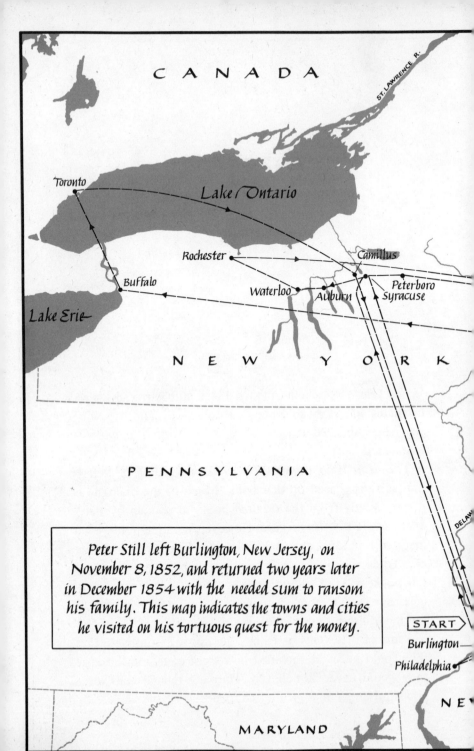

CANADA

ST. LAWRENCE R.

Toronto

Lake Ontario

Rochester

Camillus

Buffalo

Waterloo

Peterboro

Auburn

Syracuse

Lake Erie

NEW YORK

PENNSYLVANIA

DELAW

Peter Still left Burlington, New Jersey, on November 8, 1852, and returned two years later in December 1854 with the needed sum to ransom his family. This map indicates the towns and cities he visited on his tortuous quest for the money.

START

Burlington

Philadelphia

NE

MARYLAND

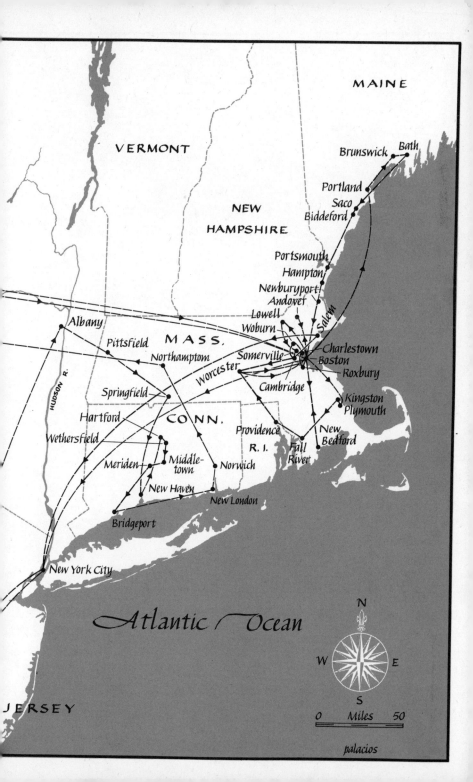

# 1

———◆———

It was a soft, hot summertime afternoon. Two boys were playing in the long shade cast by the wooden cabin. They built a roadway out of pebbles and put small sticks in the ground to fence a field. Then they looked up. There was the clacking sound of a horse's hoofs.

A white man in a gig came around the bend. When he reached the cabin he pulled on the reins, and his skinny horse stopped. For a moment he sat looking down at them. Then he said in a friendly voice, "Howdy, boys."

Peter stood up. He patted the horse's nose. "Howdy," he said shyly, speaking more to the horse than to the man.

"You like cake?" The man reached into his bag and took out two small cakes. He handed them to Peter, who promptly stuffed them into his mouth.

The man laughed. "One of those was for your brother." He handed a cake to Levin, who nibbled on it but said nothing.

"You boys here alone?"

Peter nodded. "Mama and Daddy and Mahala's in church. Grandmama too. We're little, so we don't have to go yet."

"You look like big boys to me," the man said. "How old are you?"

"Six," said Peter. "And my brother's eight."

"What's your name?"

"Peter, sir."

"*Peter!*" The man leaned back in astonishment. "Why, you are the very boys I am looking for. Peter and his brother! Glad I found you so soon! Your mammy went down to the Delaware. She asked me would I bring you to her. Give you a ride in my gig."

Peter started to climb in. But the man said, "You got any breeches? It may get cold by the river."

"Don't have no breeches," Peter said, looking down at his shirt, which hung below his knees. "This shirt is all I got."

"Well, fetch a blanket. That'll do."

Peter raced inside, took the blanket from his mother's bed. He wrapped it around him, tripped as he ran out, and fell flat in the dirt.

The man jumped from the gig. He picked Peter up, placed him on the seat, and put the horse's reins in his hands. "You like to drive?"

Peter nodded. He'd never held a horse's reins. He felt important up so high.

"What about you, boy?" the man said to Levin. "You staying, or coming?"

Levin spoke for the first time. "My mama didn't tell me nothing about no river."

"That's because she only heard about it at church. When she left home she didn't know about it."

"About what?" said Levin.

"The celebration—down by the Delaware. All kinds of food. Singing. Fireworks."

"Fireworks!" Peter exclaimed. He had no idea what fireworks was. But he knew it was something he did not want to miss.

"I'm Mr. Kincaid," the man said, picking Levin up and

swinging him into the seat beside Peter. He tucked part of the blanket around Levin's legs. Then he climbed into the gig and took the reins from Peter. "Let me start her off, boy. Otherwise, this old nag of mine might run away." He raised his arm. The whip slashed through the air above the horse's back and she took off. They jolted down the dirt road.

"Can I drive now?" Peter shouted out the words.

But Mr. Kincaid did not seem to hear. He lifted the reins, slapped them down on the horse's rump. She broke into a jerky gallop.

Peter clung hard to the edge of the seat and laughed with excitement. Here he was, high up in the world on his way to a celebration at the Delaware River. Maybe fireworks were sweet and steaming hot, like hominy grits with honey.

They galloped on, past the path in the woods that led to the white wooden church; past cabins they had never seen before; past fields framed by wooden fences. He thought of the tiny fields with stick fences that he and Levin had been making. And suddenly, for some reason, he wished they were back home, playing in front of their cabin.

Mr. Kincaid slowed the horse to a walk. Her sides were heaving in and out, and there were dark patches of sweat on her neck and shoulders.

Levin took Peter's hand and started to move off the seat.

"Where you going?" Mr. Kincaid asked, fastening his hand around Levin's thin arm.

"We don't want to go to no celebration!" Levin declared. "We want to go home!"

"I told you, boy," said Mr. Kincaid, "your mammy asked me to bring you." He clucked to the horse and she started trotting slowly. Then he took two more cakes from the bag.

This time the cake was dry in Peter's mouth, and hard to swallow.

Daylight had faded into dusk by the time they reached the river. The last edges of sunset streaked the graying sky and wavered on the darkness of the water.

The river was cluttered with boats. Some had sails, sharp white against the evening sky. There were canoes, and there were giant rowboats, each with a cabin built on top of a wooden raft.

"Where's our mama?" Levin said in a loud voice. "And our daddy? And Grandmama? And Mahala?"

"There!" Kincaid pointed to the largest boat. Men on the cabin roof leaned on the longest oar Peter had ever seen. There were more men at the front of the raft, with a shorter oar. "That's where the celebration is," Kincaid said. "On that big flatboat."

Peter squinted. It was now too dark to tell one person clearly from another. There were white hats like the one Mr. Kincaid wore. But the faces of the men on deck were erased by the gray of evening. It looked as if bodyless white hats were walking around.

"I don't hear no celebrating from that flatboat," said Levin. "No singing. Nothing."

"Maybe they're having their food," said Mr. Kincaid. "Too busy eating to sing."

He lifted the boys down, handed Levin the blanket. "You stay right here now." He unhitched the horse. "Wait for me. Don't you move, or you'll get lost and you'll never find your mammy." He led the horse away.

"I don't believe Mama's on that boat," said Levin.

"Where is she?"

"Most likely at home. And that is where we're going. Right now!"

4

"But where *is* home?" asked Peter.

"I—don't know. We come such a long way. And there was so many twists in the road. . . ."

"Maybe Mama *is* on the boat," said Peter. "With Daddy and Grandmama and Mahala. All stuffing up on roast pig and molasses pudding."

They stood debating whether or not they should run and hide—or trust that the white man would take them to their mother. Presently Mr. Kincaid returned without the horse. He gave each boy another cake and planted a hard hand on their shoulders. "Now," he announced, "to find your mammy!"

They went down to the river and across a plank that connected the shore to the deck of the boat. Peter glanced back and saw a man hitching Mr. Kincaid's horse to the gig.

"Someone's stealing your horse!" he cried out.

But Mr. Kincaid shoved them on as though he had not heard. When they reached the deck he released them. "Your mammy's below. Down that ladder."

"Mama!" Peter shrieked. He ran to the ladder leading into darkness. Then he glanced back. They were taking the plank away, pulling it onto the deck of the ship.

Mr. Kincaid was right behind them. Maybe he was coming to the celebration. Maybe he would drive them home again. All of them. His mama, daddy—

"Go on," said Mr. Kincaid. "Your mammy's waiting." With gentle pressure he shoved them forward. There was nothing to do but climb down. Mr. Kincaid was a big man, and he loomed behind them, blocking their way.

Slowly they descended into a stifling darkness that reeked of sweat and cow dung. An oil lamp hung from the ceiling. It cast a faded, swaying light on people squatting, standing, sitting on crates and burlap bags.

No one was eating. No one was singing. No one looked happy. Everyone stared straight ahead, as if each was encased in his own gloom. The only sound was that of a baby squalling.

"*Mama!*" Peter shrieked. "Mama, are you here?"

All the heads turned toward him.

The baby kept on crying.

"Mama!" Levin called out. "Where *are* you?"

Peter could hear the terror in his brother's voice.

Suddenly the boat lurched.

"We're moving," someone said.

"We got to get out of this place!" Levin shouted. "Mama ain't here." He scrambled back up the ladder.

"Where you think you're going, boy?" a rough voice said.

"We got to get off this ship, sir!" Levin cried. "Our mama ain't here!"

Peter looked up. A white man in a cap stood at the top of the steps. Then Mr. Kincaid was filling the open space, bending down toward them. His teeth smiled through the darkness. "Just found out, boys," he said, "the celebration's farther on down the river. Your mammy's there. Her and your daddy. Even your old grandmammy. All waiting for you."

"We don't want to go to no celebration!" Levin's voice was shrill. "We want to get off this here boat. We want to go home!"

"Too late now," Mr. Kincaid said. "The boat's hauled anchor."

"We want to come up on deck!" Levin shouted.

"No colored up here, boys." The man in the cap was closing a door, shutting them in. He shoved at Levin's shoulder with his foot. He had not pushed hard, but Levin, caught unawares, tumbled backward.

He lay at the bottom of the ladder, not moving.

Peter screamed. He knelt beside his brother. "Are you hurt, Levin?"

Slowly Levin got to his knees.

The dark faces in the rocking lamplight were watching. No one spoke. No one came to help.

"No, I ain't hurt," Levin said.

"What're we going to do?" Peter whispered.

"Do? There's nothing to do. We're trapped."

## 2

A figure came from the shadows—an old woman. She stood for a moment, looking down at them. Then she sat and put her arms around Peter. She was very thin; her skin hung in dark folds around her neck. She smelled like his grandmama. He wondered, through his fear, whether all old people had the same dried-up smell.

"Now, tell Mother Grace," she said, "what has happened to you boys?"

They told her, one talking, then the other. And Mother Grace listened hard. When they had finished, she made her pronouncement, "Seems to me, you two boys been stolen by that Kincaid. Kidnaped. When you get off this boat, you must run away. Find your way back home."

"But—how?" cried Peter.

A man's deep voice spoke out from the back. "Travel in the night. Hide if you see a white man. Don't trust no white man. Ever." The final sentences were delivered with all the fervor of a preacher in church.

"But how can we get home?" said Levin loudly. "We don't even know where home *is!*"

The question was answered by silence.

Peter began to cry. First he sniffled, trying to hold back his tears. But they came, leaking out of his eyes. Then he burst into gasping sobs.

"Don't cry, Peter," Levin said. Then he too started to cry. Mother Grace sat with an arm around each of them, holding them to her and crooning in a soothing way, until they fell asleep.

Hours later Peter was startled awake. Where was he? What was this dark, smelly, rocking place? Who were these strangers sitting, lying all around? Most of them sleeping.

He was about to scream out in terror. Then he remembered.

His brother was curled up beside him on the floor, asleep. But the old lady, Mother Grace, was awake, and she smiled at him. Inside her stretched lips there was darkness; she had no teeth. He was frightened of her, until she asked in a soft voice, "Feeling better, son, now that you slept a little?"

He sat up straight. "I don't feel good at all," he said. "I want my mama."

"Sure you do," said Mother Grace. "Sure you do, child." Then she asked him where he and his brother had come from. "I been down in this hold so long," she said, "I don't rightly know where we're at."

"The white man, he took us to the Delaware River," Peter said. "That's all I know."

"You don't know where you're from, boy? The state where you're from?"

Peter shook his head. "All I know is how to get to church, and the fields around our cabin."

Mother Grace looked thoughtful. He could see her face in the swaying light of the oil lamp. He could watch her thinking hard. Finally she said, "Being you don't know where you're from, might as well be from a free state. I do believe the Delaware River run past Philadelphia. Leastways, some river do." She looked at him and said the word slowly: "Phil-a-del-fee-yah. Say that after me, child."

He repeated the syllables slowly.

"Good," said Mother Grace. "Now, anyone asks you or your brother where you're from, you tell 'em Phil-a-del-fee-yah. Or the countryside nearabouts there. That way they'll know you're a free nigger and not no slave."

"But I am a slave," said Peter. "My mama and daddy are slaves. My grandmama—"

"Hush, child." The old woman put her hand over his mouth. "You do what Mother Grace tells you. It may be no help. But it can't do no hurt."

Peter nodded. He was feeling hungry again. He wondered whether Mr. Kincaid had any more cakes. And remembering the cakes, all the anger and fear rushed back inside him. He had been tricked with those cakes. And now he was here in the bottom of this boat, going—

"Where are we?" he cried out to Mother Grace. "Where are we going?"

"I figger we must be on the Ohio River by now," the old woman said. "Maybe passing Cave-in-Rock." She made her voice low and shaky. "A pirate's den!" And she told him about farmers bringing their crops down river on flatboats . . . passing the large river-front sign that read: "Wilson's Liquor Vault and House for Entertainment." But when a farmer docked his boat and entered the mouth of the cave, he was pounced on by Bully Wilson and his band of outlaws. At that, the climax, Mother Grace laughed loudly, a creaky sound. Peter laughed too, just a little.

She told him other river stories, even better tales than the ones his grandmama told. It helped him to forget his hunger and his fear.

Presently Levin woke up. Mother Grace told *him* about Philadelphia. Then she thought out another plan. "Looks like this Mr. Kincaid is taking you boys *somewhere*. You go 'long with him. No use you running away if you don't know which way to run to. This white man, he knows where you are from. Likely he won't tell you, if you ask him. But you stick close by him when he is talking to other white folks. He'll let it slip out, where he took you from. And," she concluded, "soon as you know where you're from—you can figger out how to get back there."

Another woman spoke. She sat near the ladder, nursing her baby. "Mother Grace, why you fill these two children full of fool ideas? This white man, he'll sell them down South, and they'll never get back nowhere!"

Suddenly the trap door opened. There was a square of daylight, and two buckets were lowered by ropes.

"Breakfast!" said Mother Grace in a sour voice. "Corn bread one week old. And sassafras tea."

They passed the buckets around. Each person took a piece of bread and a cupful of tea. Peter wanted to take more bread and hide it till later. He wanted to drink more of the lukewarm tea. But he did as the others had done; he hung the cup on the nail of the bucket and shoved it over to Levin. Maybe Mr. Kincaid would come fetch them out soon. Then Peter would ask for some cakes.

But Mr. Kincaid did not come. Time dragged like a man walking down the road in chains. Everything Peter's thoughts settled on, he found frightening. He wanted to cry and keep on crying. But not in front of these strangers. Levin had grown so still it was almost as if he were not there at all. Maybe keeping quiet was Levin's way of trying not to cry.

There was a wooden bucket in the back. Peter soon

found out what that was for. It was what smelled up the whole place. That and sweat, and people throwing up from the rocking of the boat in the river current.

Presently Peter fell asleep again. He woke up screaming, "Mama, where *are* you? Mama. . . ."

But there was only Mother Grace to hold him against her skinny flat chest. "Hush, child," she crooned. "Hush. . . ."

Finally, after the buckets of food and tea or water had been lowered four times—which meant, said Mother Grace, a passage of two days and two nights—finally the boat stopped. The trap door was opened, and a white man shouted, "All up on deck."

Peter climbed stiffly up the ladder behind Levin. It was nighttime. When he stood on deck he took deep breaths of the soft, clean air and looked up at the high stars. They were the same stars he could see from his bed by the cabin window at home. He would often lie looking up at them . . . these same stars. Now they gave him hope that he and Levin were not too far from home.

"Well, here you are, boys!" It was Mr. Kincaid, with his friendly voice and his firm grasp on their arms. "I been looking all over this boat for you. I got a wagon waiting to take you to your mammy."

"You got any more cakes?" said Peter.

"Well, sure, boy. I surely do. I been saving them for you." He gave them several cakes. Peter gobbled them down. Levin did too.

Mr. Kincaid laughed. "Looks like you won't be getting to that celebration any too soon. You hungry, boys?"

"We only got bread and tea down there," said Peter.

The white man laughed again. "Well, we will rectify that soon enough!" he exclaimed.

A plank now lay between the ship and the shore. They crossed it behind Mr. Kincaid. Several wagons were waiting.

"We're on the last lap of our journey, boys," he said as he hoisted them into one of the wagons. There was a basket—of food! Chicken legs. Apples. Corn bread. Cucumbers. Cakes. Peter and Levin stuffed themselves fast and full. Then, rocked by the rhythmic jolting of the cart, they burrowed down into the straw and continued their nighttime sleep.

"Levin! Wake up! Look!"

It was daylight. Peter had crawled to the back of the wagon and sat staring out in astonishment.

They were clattering down a wide road made, not of dirt, but of stones set evenly in place. And this road was lined with houses; some were wood, and some were made of long reddish bricks. Peter had never seen so many houses—and so many people—all in one place. Men and women, even children, walking about in fine-looking clothes.

Levin had crawled to the back of the wagon, and he too lay staring out in wonder. "This is a big place!" he declared. "Maybe it's Philadelphia!"

Other wagons rattled along the stone-paved street, as well as gigs and buggies drawn by handsome horses. Some buildings had letters above the front door, and huge front windows. "Shops!" said Levin. "You can go in there and buy different things—if you have money."

Suddenly Peter let out a shattered cry. "The blanket! Mama's blanket!"

They stared at each other in despair. It was not just that they had left their blanket on the boat. They had left the only thing they had that tied them to their home, the

*13*

blanket they had taken straight from the bed in which Mama and Daddy slept every night. Remembering the blanket led to a new thought: his parents, Grandmama, and Mahala coming home from church on Sunday evening . . . not finding them. "Maybe they went off to the woods to gather berries," Mama might say. "They'll be home before dark." But when she went into the cabin— when she saw that her blanket was missing—Mama would start to worry. And when they did not come home at all that Sunday night. . . .

"They'll know we was stolen!" Peter cried. "Or maybe they'll think we was killed and wrapped in the blanket and thrown away in the woods someplace."

The new weight of his family's sorrow sat inside him, a sorrow too heavy for tears.

Presently the wagon stopped before a fine-looking house made of red bricks. A white boy about Levin's size stood by the door.

Mr. Kincaid came to the back of the wagon and said in a cheerful voice, "Well, boys, we've had a long trip. But we're finally here."

"Where?" said Levin.

Mr. Kincaid seemed surprised. "Didn't I tell you I was bringing you to your mammy?"

"Is she here?" Peter cried, hope rocketing within him.

"You'll see her in just a few more minutes," said Mr. Kincaid. "First I want Mr. Fisher to meet you. He lives in this house. Let him look you over all he wants. But don't say nothing. If he asks you a question, I'll give the answer. Don't speak unless I give you the sign to do so. That sign will be a nod from me. You understand, boys?"

"We don't want to see no white man!" Peter shouted. "We want to see our mama."

"Quiet!" The word was like a whip through the air. Then Mr. Kincaid smiled, and all the sharpness disappeared. "Look, you do as I say . . . just as I say . . . and if you pass the test, I promise you, this very morning you will be eating breakfast with your mammy."

# 3

"John," Mr. Kincaid called to the boy at the front door. "Your daddy home?"

"Yes, sir. I'll fetch him." The boy disappeared into the house.

"You know, son," Mr. Kincaid said to Levin, "here we've been traveling all this way and I don't even know your name."

Levin stared straight ahead, saying nothing.

But Peter remembered the white man's words: *if* they were good . . . if they passed the test . . . they would see their mama. "His name is Levin," Peter said quickly.

Kincaid nodded. "And Levin is ten years old. Correct?"

"No, sir," said Peter. "Eight."

Mr. Kincaid frowned. "How could that be? This is 1806. Your mammy told me her oldest son was born in the year 1796. That would make Levin ten years old. Right?" Although he asked it as a question, his voice was flat and firm, giving the answer: Levin was ten years old.

A tall and handsome white man had come to the door of the house. He stood with his hand on his son's shoulder, waiting for them.

"You follow me now," said Mr. Kincaid, lifting the boys from the wagon. "And remember, don't say nothing unless I give you the nod to speak."

As he had directed, they walked behind him to the front door.

"Morning, Mr. Fisher," said Mr. Kincaid.

"Morning," said Mr. Fisher abruptly. He looked down at Peter and Levin, frowning a little. "These the best you could get me?"

"Indeed, they are the best!" said Mr. Kincaid, sounding insulted. "Strong and healthy. They'll grow into fine bucks."

"Sure," said Mr. Fisher. "They'll grow, all right. After a few years of feeding them up. But it won't be *my* food they'll be growing on! I told you, Kincaid, I wanted two boys ready to work in the brickyard now. And that means two boys ten years old, or more."

"This one *is* ten," said Kincaid, putting a hand on Levin's shoulder.

"*Ten!*" Mr. Fisher raised Levin's chin gently, and in the kindest voice he asked, "How old are you, son?"

Levin glanced at Mr. Kincaid—who did not nod. Instead, he frowned just a little.

"Don't—know, sir," Levin said.

Peter felt relief wash through him. If Levin had said "eight," if he had angered Mr. Kincaid, they would never get to see their mama.

"His own mother told me the boy was born in 1796," said Mr. Kincaid patiently. "If she don't know his right age, I don't know who does."

Mr. Fisher felt Levin's upper arms. "Not much muscle," he said. He asked Levin to open his mouth, and he prodded with his forefinger at the boy's teeth. Then he squatted, felt Levin's calves. When he stood up he said, "I'll give you a hundred and fifty for this one. Don't want the other one at all."

Kincaid exploded in anger. "Look here, Mr. Fisher, you

said two boys and I brought you two boys. You said two hundred a piece. And that's what I want. That's what they're worth, every penny of it. In a few years they'll be worth double the price. If you keep them on till they're full grown, they'll bring a thousand each—or more, the way prices keep shooting up!"

A white woman came out to join them. She was a stout, freckle-faced lady. For a moment she stood listening to the men as they argued about price. Then she said in a soft voice, "Mr. Fisher, while you two gentlemen discuss business affairs, why don't you send the boys in for some breakfast?"

Mr. Fisher nodded. "John," he said to the white boy, "take them in to Aunt Betty."

"Kitchen's to the back," the boy said. "This way." As they followed him down a dirt path to the back of the big house, John asked, "Where you from?"

Levin did not answer.

But Peter wanted to say something. They had been warned not to speak to Mr. Fisher. But Mr. Kincaid had said nothing about the son of Mr. Fisher. Besides, this boy sounded friendly.

"Philadelphia," Peter said loudly. Somehow saying it loudly made it sound more true. "We're from Philadelphia."

"That's a long way from here." The white boy seemed impressed. "This is the kitchen." He led them into a large room with an iron stove in one corner. A black woman stood by the long wooden table, kneading dough.

"Aunt Betty, my mother says to give these boys some breakfast."

She smiled, wiped her hands on her apron, and came toward them. "So you're the two new ones. Would you like some grits and bacon? And nice hot biscuits?"

"Yes, ma'am," said Peter. Levin stared at Aunt Betty and said nothing.

As she set the food on the table, Peter kept looking toward the door. When was his mama coming in?

*If you pass the test*, Mr. Kincaid had said, *I promise you this very morning you will be eating breakfast with your mammy.*

*Had* they passed the test? What *was* the test? Here was breakfast all set out on the table. But nothing more had been said about their mother eating with them. Maybe she was busy. Maybe Mr. Fisher had put her to work while she was waiting for them to get here. She would come to the kitchen when she had finished.

"Sit, boys, and eat," Aunt Betty said. "Never saw two young 'uns didn't want my hot biscuits!"

The biscuits were good, and Peter was hungry. But somehow he found them hard to swallow.

What if Mama was not here? Suddenly the full meaning of Mr. Fisher's words fell on him like a heavy rock. *I'll give you a hundred and fifty for this one. Don't want the other one at all.*

Levin was for sale! He was being bought by Mr. Fisher. *Don't want the other one at all.*

What would happen to him, Peter? Without his brother? Where would they send him? Would they kill him? His heart started pounding. His insides were churning. He felt he might throw up right there on the kitchen floor.

After a while Mr. Fisher entered the kitchen, followed by Mr. Kincaid.

"Well, boys." Mr. Kincaid was smiling. "It was a long trip, but we finally found your mammy." He looked at Aunt Betty. "Them's two fine sons you got there. Take care of them now." He turned on his heel and walked out.

*19*

Peter screamed. "NO!" He ran after Mr. Kincaid and grabbed his shirt. "No, sir, please, that ain't our mama. That's Aunt Betty. That ain't our mama. Please, sir, oh, please take us back where you got us. Please, sir, don't leave us here in this place."

Kincaid kept on walking. And Peter kept on shrieking, clinging to Kincaid's shirt, his arm, his belt.

Rough hands pulled him away. A sharp slap on each cheek. Peter looked up. The white man towered above him. "No more of this, boy," Mr. Fisher bellowed. "Aunt Betty's your mammy now. And you belong to me. Next time you forget that, I'll teach you with a whip."

"Please," Peter screamed, clutching now at Mr. Fisher's shirt. "Oh, please, sir—he stole us from our mama. My brother's not ten. He's eight. I'm six. He lied to you, sir. Please, sir, find out where he stole us from. And send us home!"

Mr. Fisher answered with a heavy blow that knocked Peter to the ground.

The boy scrambled to his feet. Mr. Kincaid had jumped into the wagon. He lashed his horse, which started into a jerky lope.

"PLEASE!" Peter ran after the wagon. "Tell us where our mama is. Please. . . . Waaaaait." He stood in the street, his body wracked with strangled sobbing; as the wagon turned a corner and disappeared.

People stared at him. He didn't care. He and Levin had not found out where they came from! How could they ever get home?

A hand clamped around Peter's arm and pulled him along. Mr. Fisher was cursing at him, each word like a whiplash. He dragged Peter into the house. Slammed the front door. Threw the boy to the floor.

"Listen here, you nigger! I paid a hundred and fifty goddamn dollars for you. And one hundred and fifty-five for your brother. If I ever hear you say again, to me or to anyone, that you was stolen—I will break your black neck. You understand that, boy?" He lifted his foot, kicked Peter in the ribs, and left the room.

Peter got up. He ran out the front door, around to the back of the house, and into the kitchen. Levin was there. Peter hurtled into his brother's arms. "What we gonna do?" he kept sobbing over and over. "We been sold. What we gonna do?"

Aunt Betty came over, lifted Peter in her arms, and sat, holding him in her lap like a baby. She rocked back and forth and crooned to him as Mother Grace had done. "Hush, child . . . hush." But he didn't want them—not either of them, Mother Grace or Aunt Betty. He wanted his *own* mother. He wanted to be back home.

Presently Mr. Fisher and his son came into the kitchen.

Peter had stopped crying. Levin had not cried at all. Both boys sat by the kitchen table, sunk in a quicksand of gloom.

"The older boy is ten," said Fisher to Aunt Betty. "He can work in the yard, starting tomorrow. But the little one's only six. You can use him in the kitchen. Send him for the cows. Let him help in the house. Keep him busy." Then he turned to Peter. "I didn't want you at all, boy. I ordered two ten-year-old niggers. Not a runt of six. I only bought you out of the kindness of my heart—so as not to see you separated from your brother. But don't you make me regret it, boy. You understand me?"

Peter looked up, his eyes hard. "Yes, Master," he said.

# 4

---◆►---

The white boy, John, took a biscuit from the table. He nibbled at it, watching Peter closely. And he looked as sorrowful as Peter himself.

As Mr. Fisher started to leave, John said, "Father, we learned in school that Philadelphia's the capital city of Pennsylvania."

"That's right, son."

"And Pennsylvania's a free state. No slaves there."

Mr. Fisher turned, scowling a little. He waited.

"Well," said John, "these two boys are from Philadelphia. They're not slaves. Mr. Kincaid stole them and brought them down to Kentucky. He had no right to sell these boys to you."

Mr. Fisher looked at his son, his eyes like bullets. "Now who," he inquired in a flat voice, his words spaced wide, "who told you that, John? That these two boys were stolen?"

"Why, Peter did, Father. He told me how—"

"Look, John," Mr. Fisher said—but he was staring straight at Peter. "I bought these two boys. I paid a good price for them. I got the bill of sale. And I will thrash the life out of anyone who says these boys were stolen."

"But why, Father?"

"Because—" Mr. Fisher wheeled, turned all his anger onto his son. "If I ever want to get shut of these boys, it'd spoil the sale if anyone thought there was problems about ownership. There is to be nothing said," he thundered, "—ever again—about where these boys are from. Or that they were stolen. Does everyone understand that right and clear?"

John stared back at his father for a long moment. Then he gave a slight nod.

"Free!" Mr. Fisher spat out a laugh. "They're better off here than if they *were* free and growing up shiftless lazy with no one to look after them, take care of them." He started once again for the door. And once again he turned. "Even if Kincaid did steal them, so were all the Negroes stolen at first. Come, John."

Slowly the boy followed his father from the kitchen.

Aunt Betty went to the door, and when father and son were out of earshot, she turned and said to Peter and Levin, "Now I will teach you two boys a lesson of more use than anything young Master John will ever learn in school!" In a low, clear voice she sang two lines: "Got one mind for the boss to see,/Got another mind for what I know is me."

The boys looked at her, expressionless.

"You learn that song," she said. "And never forget it. The meaning is, you can say your own thoughts—be your own self—around your own kind. Though even some of *them*'s not to be trusted. I'm thinking special of the house servants. Not *me*, not anyone in *this* house. But in some houses you'll find niggers what act as spies for the master. So go soft around them. Don't say nothing you wouldn't say to a white man. And"—she spaced her words to make each one sink in slowly—"don't say nothing to a white man that he would not want to hear. If you do, it'll get you nothing but a body full of scars from the whip. You understand me, boys?"

They nodded.

"You're not bad off here," Aunt Betty said. "I'll look after you like you were my own. And Master Fisher—if you don't rile him—he's a lot better than most. He'll work you hard, but he's kind. He won't whip you without cause. And Mrs. Fisher, she's a good woman. She don't use the whip at all. She won't kick you. She just hits and scolds, like she does her own two boys, John and Sidney."

"Sidney!" Peter exclaimed, his face lighting up. "That's my mama's name! Sidney!"

"You're sure?" said Aunt Betty. "Thought that was a man's name, Sidney."

"It's my mama's name," Peter insisted. "That's what they call her. And that's what's her name. Even my daddy calls her Sidney."

"And our daddy's name," Levin spoke up, "is Levin. I'm the firstborn son, so I was named after my daddy. Levin!"

"We know their names," Peter exulted. "That will help us to find our way back home."

"What's their second name?" Aunt Betty asked.

They stared at her blankly.

"Slaves like me," she explained, "we got no second names of our own. I'm Aunt Betty Fisher. But that's just to show who I belong to. If I get sold I'll have another second name, the name of my new master. But—if your mama and daddy are free, must be they have their own second name. Maybe *that* would help you to find them, if you can get back to Philadelphia."

Peter and Levin said nothing more. They did not know

what second name their parents had, but they did know that their parents were slaves.

Peter was about to tell this to Aunt Betty, but he caught the words before they came out. If everyone thought that he and Levin came from Philadelphia—if everyone thought they had been born free—maybe this would help them to *get* free. Somehow. Someday.

Later that morning a handsome, heavy-set black man stopped at the kitchen door and called, "Boy here name of Levin?"

"He's here," said Aunt Betty. "Go 'long now, child." She gave him a gentle shove toward the door.

"Go where?" Levin cried fearfully.

"I want to go too," said Peter loudly. "Where my brother goes, I want to go too."

"He's going to the brickyard," said Aunt Betty. "But, Peter, you're still too little to work there. You stay and help me cut the beans and shell the peas."

"What's the brickyard?" asked Levin and Peter together.

"Master Fisher's a mason. He owns the brickyard out in back. Got fifteen slaves working there. You go 'long with Charles, and you'll soon see what's a brickyard."

"And," said Charles, "if you don't come quick, you'll see a slave get the whip."

"They not gonna whip me!" said Levin, defiant.

"Not you," said Charles. "It's me they'll whip for taking so long to fetch you to the yard." He held out his hand in a friendly way. And Levin slowly went toward him.

As they walked out the door Peter cried, "I'm going too!" And he ran after them.

"You're a fool, boy," Charles said to Peter. "Right now you got the only happy time a slave can ever know. You're too little for hard work. You'll get light work, and lots of time for play. Stay away from the brickyard, boy, till they send you there. That time'll come only too soon."

"I—I'll tell you about it when I get back," Levin said to Peter. "You go to Aunt Betty now. I'll see you in the kitchen later."

Peter looked at his brother, who suddenly seemed to *be* ten years old.

"Go 'long, now," Levin said sternly.

Peter turned and walked slowly back to the kitchen.

That afternoon the Fisher boys, John and his younger brother Sidney, took Peter to the plantation their father rented from the widow, Mrs. Russell. It would be Peter's job to visit this plantation every day. He would pick vegetables from the garden to take home to Aunt Betty, and he would help bring in the cows from the pasture.

The plantation lay a mile and a half from Lexington, and the three boys were tired by the time they reached it. They stopped to rest in the shade of a tree. Suddenly John said, "Let's take Peter to Ashland. He can tell his story to Mr. Clay—how he was stolen from his mammy. Mr. Clay will help him get home again."

"Mr. Clay?" said Peter. "Who is Mr. Clay?"

"Senator Henry Clay," John told him. The most important man in the county. He's been to Washington. He knows the rules of this country, and he's a lawyer besides. He can *make* my father send you home to Philadelphia."

"Where is he at?" said Peter eagerly.

"His plantation's just across from the one our daddy rents." Sidney got to his feet. Then he looked down at Peter. "But if he does send you home, you mustn't tell our daddy it was John and me who took you to see Senator Clay."

"I never will tell," Peter promised. "When I get home, I will thank you in my prayers every night. But I never will tell no one but Jesus how I got there."

As he entered the plantation called Ashland, Peter felt that he now knew where Jesus lived and what heaven was like.

They walked down a large, circular roadway with flat green grass and flower beds set out in the center. As far as he could see on either side there stretched peaceful green, flowers, shrub fences, and tall trees backed by soft blue sky. The most amazing splendor was straight ahead—Clay's plantation home. It was, like the Fisher house, made of bricks. But this house was two and a half stories high, with one-story wings at each end. The windows were filled with the shine of afternoon sunlight.

As they stood there a white boy about Peter's age ran out the front door and down the steps.

"Ted!" John Fisher called to him, and the boy came over.

"Is your daddy here?" John asked.

"What you want with my daddy?"

"This here boy was stolen from his house in Philadelphia," Sidney announced. "Philadelphia's a free state, so this nigger ain't even a slave. We want to ask Senator Clay how to send him back home again."

"Me *and* my brother," Peter said. "He was stolen too."

"But listen," John warned Ted Clay, "this all must be kept a secret. If my daddy finds out what we done, he'll skin us alive."

"Why?" asked Ted.

"Because my daddy, he paid good money for these two niggers," John explained. "He don't want to hear about how they was born free and how they was stolen."

"Well, you're right to come to *my* daddy!" Ted said proudly. "He's not in the house. Let's look out back."

As they ran along a flower-edged path, Peter suddenly remembered the preacher-sounding words of the black man in the dark hold of the boat. *Don't trust no white man. Ever.*

But this Senator Clay must be different. He would help them. His own son had said so.

"Maybe your father is in one of the ice houses," Sidney suggested.

"What's ice houses?" Peter asked.

"I'll show you," said Ted. They walked on. Then Ted Clay pointed toward two of the strangest looking buildings Peter had ever seen: they were round and small, with tall roofs that came to a point on top. When the boys went inside Peter gasped, for the weather suddenly changed from a steamy, hot summer afternoon to winter. The houses were filled with huge chunks of ice which, Ted told him, were indeed brought there in the wintertime. Men cut blocks of ice from the river and carted them to the ice houses in wagons.

"But why?" asked Peter.

"See that tunnel?" Sidney pointed. "The melted ice runs along underground to the dairy. Senator Clay owns thirty cows. He sells milk to the Phoenix Hotel in Lexington. The ice house is to keep the milk cold. The Phoenix Hotel won't pay for sour milk."

They continued to search for Senator Clay. They stopped in the smokehouse, where thick slabs of bacon and whole skinned hogs hung by iron hooks from the ceiling. They looked in Mrs. Clay's greenhouse, where an amazement of flowers, ferns, and shrubs flourished under a roof which, like the windows of the Big House, was—said Ted—made of something called glass.

There were barns, a chicken house, a coach house. And then they saw a tall, thin man striding from the stable.

"There's my father," cried Ted, and he ran down the path.

The other three boys followed more slowly.

When Peter stood before Senator Clay, he felt certain that this man would help him. The Senator looked something like God. His hair was white, his forehead high, and his eyes were an unusual gray. He had a large nose, his mouth was long and thin, his skin pale. And his voice, when he spoke, was low and gentle.

"My son tells me you've been kidnaped," he said, and he put his hand on Peter's shoulder. He was smiling a little.

Peter did not know what "kidnaped" meant. He answered politely, "Me and my brother was stolen, sir."

"Are you sure?" said Senator Clay.

"Oh, yes, sir," Peter exclaimed. And he told the Senator how he and Levin had been tricked by Kincaid. He added that they came from the free state of Philadelphia. "We are not slaves!" he declared stoutly.

Once again the Senator smiled, just a little. Then he looked off toward the distant fields where the grass was flecked with the tiny shapes of cattle grazing. "I'll look into the matter," he said finally. "It may take some time. In the meantime, none of you boys must mention a word of this to anyone. Otherwise, Mr. Fisher may do as he says— thrash the life out of young Peter here. So it will be our secret. Right, boys?"

"Yes, sir," they chorused.

Then Senator Clay strode off down the pebbled pathway.

As the boys stood looking after him, Ted exclaimed proudly, "I told you my daddy would fix things!"

# 5

---◆---

Three years later, Peter and Levin still belonged to the mason John Fisher, who lived on Main Street in Lexington, Kentucky.

It was not that Senator Clay had forgotten about Peter and the promise he had given the boy. Indeed, he had little chance to forget. Several times a week, after Peter had finished work picking vegetables or bringing in the cows for Mr. Fisher, he crossed the road and entered the special world of Ashland.

Clay was often away from home, in Washington, or elsewhere. And when he was at Ashland he usually remained in the Big House, in his office or library. But on the rare occasions when Peter was able to confront him, the boy always found Clay to be kind, sympathetic, and understanding. "First we must find out where you were stolen from," the Senator would tell Peter, "so we can send you back there. No use to raise the issue with Mr. Fisher yet."

And Peter knew from his own very painful experience how true this was. His back was laced with scars from the whip. And each time the whipping had been for the same reason. He had, on the whole, been treated well by the Fishers. But during the first year, he and Levin had slept on the floor in the Fishers' bedroom. Often, late at night, as they lay under the bed or the bureau Peter and Levin would "remember together." In low whispers they relived memories of their mama, their daddy, their sister Mahala, their grandmama, the cabin, the church, the nearby woods. And by so doing they kept the memories from fading. Sometimes, however, they also whispered about the terrible afternoon on which they were kidnaped by Mr. Kincaid. And if Master Fisher happened to be lying awake and overheard such conversation, he would rise from his bed like a demon. He would drag the boys out, whip them, and kick them, all the while shouting that they were his property and he had the right and the power to quiet their tongues forever.

After the first year, the boys were sent to live in the slave cabins out back of the main house. Here they had more privacy for their rememberings. But by this time their memories had become so mixed with fantasies that it was hard to tell the true from the imagined.

Although—as far as Peter could see—Senator Henry Clay never did "look into the matter" of where they had come from, the hope that something *might* happen was, in itself, a help. It gave young Peter quite a different inner attitude from that of the other slave boys he grew up with. He became completely convinced that he had been born somewhere near Philadelphia and, consequently, had been born free. Therefore, it was logical that somehow, someday, he would find his way back home. And he would be free once more.

In the meantime, it seemed sensible to do his jobs as well as he could, to be pleasant and cheerful, avoid whippings, and prepare himself for the day when he would be as free as any white boy in the land.

Early on a hot August morning, Mr. Fisher announced to Peter that, since he was now nine years old, he would work henceforth in the brickyard as an "off-bearer."

*31*

The decree sent Peter's spirits plummeting. No more easy afternoons on the plantation or playing with the slave children at Ashland. His childhood now was over, as his brother's had been that long-ago morning when Charles came to the kitchen and took Levin off to the brickyard.

Peter had visited the brickyard several times, but what he saw there made him so angry and sorrowful that he tended to avoid the place. Levin, in fact, had given him instructions to do so. "With the fires going, and the cow-hide whips, it is worse than any hell the preacher shouts about. You keep clear of that brickyard, Peter. As long as you can."

On his first afternoon in the yard, Peter was given a swift initiation into horror. *He* had to lash Charles with a cowhide whip.

Levin explained the "rules" to his brother.

Top man in the brickyard was a slave named Big Jim, who worked as a molder, the most skilled and difficult job in the yard. It was also Big Jim's job to see to it that all the boys and men working under him fulfilled their quota so that the Fisher Brickyard could turn out 10,000 bricks a day. If anyone slackened on his particular part of the job, Big Jim was permitted by Fisher to inflict any punishment he chose.

Big Jim's favorite form of punishment was called "standing in the wheelbarrow." The culprit was forced to climb into a barrow, put a foot on each wheel, and then reach over and grasp a handle in each hand. As he stood in this ludicrous and exposed position, one of the off-bearers, the youngest boys in the yard, had to whip the victim.

On this, Peter's first afternoon, it was Charles who had aroused the molder's wrath. And it was Peter who was "honored" by having to inflict the first blows.

Peter had come to love Charles, who was kind to him

and listened with sympathy to the stories of his family and the cabin he had come from somewhere near Philadelphia. How could he now hit this man with a whip? Appalled, he looked down at the fierce, snakelike thong in his hand.

"Hit him with all your strength!" Big Jim shouted out.

"How many times?" Peter asked weakly.

"He gets twenty-four lashes in all," said Big Jim. "When your strength gives out, hand your whip to another off-bearer. And if the man moves or cries out, we start the counting all over again."

Peter lifted the whip into the air. He was trembling. The ground swayed before him. He lowered his arm. "I can't," he whispered.

He received a blow on the back that sent him sprawling to the ground.

Big Jim was laughing as he hauled Peter to his feet and placed the whip in his hand again. Other slaves gathered around to watch. This did not happen every day—the breaking in of a new boy.

There was laughter; there was cheering, jeering. Then Levin was beside him. "If you don't do it, Peter, someone else will. You'll end up in the wheelbarrow yourself. And that's not going to help Charles any."

Peter lifted the whip. He slashed it through the air and brought it down hard, not on Charles's rump but on the wooden edge of the wheelbarrow.

There was a whistling sound, and a slash of pain across his own back. "Goddamn you, hit that nigger," Big Jim bellowed.

Charles cried out, "Hit me, boy. Get it done with."

Blindly Peter raised the whip. For a moment he turned, as if to hit out at Big Jim. But he saw the terror in Levin's face.

"Hit me!" Charles cried out again.

And Peter brought the whip down. It lashed against Charles's bare back.

Peter screamed. Then he dropped the whip and ran to the corner of the yard, where he started to vomit.

Levin ran over to him. Peter was sobbing. "We got to get out of this place." The words burst from him: "We got to find our way back home."

Big Jim never again asked Peter to whip anyone. Nor was the boy ever whipped, for he never gave cause for a whipping. He did his work quietly and well. The stroke he had inflicted on Charles's back seemed to have slashed into his own soul. For several weeks he did not smile or laugh, and spoke only when someone spoke to him.

Finally, however, his normally cheerful, outgoing spirit returned. As Levin put it, "Peter's self came back inside him." And, as the youngest boy in the brickyard, he became something of a favorite among the men who worked there. They were pleased with Peter's constant questions about their work. He did not, of course, tell them—or anyone—that he had decided to learn all he could about brick making, so that when he was free he would have a trade and could make his own living.

There was little enough to learn about his own job as off-bearer. The bearers worked in pairs, and each pair had to cart off 3,000 bricks a day. The first few days, as he staggered back and forth wheeling his barrow of heavy molds, with the broiling August sun pressing down on the brickyard, Peter thought he would surely die of heat, thirst, and exhaustion.

But by the end of the week, his muscles had firmed up and he could cart off as many bricks as his brother. By then, however, he thought he would surely die of boredom

—which was another reason he tried to find out what he could about how bricks were made.

It was the molder's job which interested him most. Full of admiration, he would stand by Big Jim's table and watch as Jim took a huge handful of clay from the pile on the table, formed it into a mass somewhat the shape of the mold, then forced it into the mold, striking off the extra clay with a plane. Sometimes Jim gave him some of this leftover clay to play with, and Peter would fashion little figures from it. Mostly he made animals—horses, pigs, and cows. But on one Sunday afternoon when the brickyard was closed, he made a whole family of clay: Mama, Daddy, Mahala, Grandmama, and two small boys. He was playing with them in the backyard when he saw Mr. Fisher coming toward him. Quickly he mashed the family into a mound of clay, terrified that Mr. Fisher would see he was still "remembering."

Time dragged by. Yet, when Peter looked back, it seemed to have moved quickly. Each day was much like the one before, and the one before it—until a certain springtime afternoon when Peter was thirteen.

News crackled through the slave quarters—news regarded with dread by every man, woman, and child owned by John Fisher. Master Fisher was moving to Cincinnati. He was selling his brickyard and all his slaves except Aunt Betty.

The Fisher slaves were regarded by others as being well off. They had enough to eat, enough to wear, and the Fishers rarely whipped them.

It was hard to think that any of them could fare better under a new master. Families might be split up. Some might be taken to the Deep South—those two words alone were enough to bring a chill of terror. The Deep South: land of cruel overseers, strange sicknesses, rattlesnakes.

And to Peter and Levin, the idea of being sold cut off a lifeline of hope. Since Senator Clay's promise to find out where they were from had brought no results, the boys had come to believe—or at least tried to believe—that somehow, someday, some way their parents would meet up with Mr. Kincaid and would learn where he had taken them. Then Mama or Daddy would come to find them and bring them back home.

But now—if they were to be sold—!

And they might even be separated!

As the weeks went by and one Fisher slave after another was sold, the peril grew more real for Peter and Levin. And at last Peter understood why Fisher had gone to such lengths to keep the kidnaping story quiet. No one wanted to buy the two brothers. The story *had* spread. Fisher's clear title to these two boys was cloudy, and that fact alone was enough to frighten off any buyer.

The Fisher slave quarters were almost empty. Levin and Peter now lived alone in a cabin which they had shared with ten others. The space and the privacy would have been pleasurable, except that the cabin was now pervaded by their fear. How long could they remain together? To whom would they be sold? Where would they be sent?

# 6

At the end of September the answer came.

Fisher had finally found a buyer for his two boys.

The brothers would remain together, in Lexington, and they would continue to work in a brickyard. But—their new master would be the drunken tyrant Nat Gist.

"I didn't want to sell you to old Nattie," John Fisher told the boys, rather shamefaced. "But he was the only one who offered anything at all. And then it was only $450. I could have made double that on the auction block. But I like you boys. I sacrificed a good profit so you two could stay together."

"Thank you, Master Fisher," Levin said.

Peter said nothing at all. It was hard to give thanks for being *sold*. Yet he felt light with relief, for he and Levin would not be separated.

Nat Gist was a short, stout, gray-haired man in his fifties. He lived alone in a small brick house on Dutch Street, and owned a five-acre brickyard and twenty slaves. Peter knew one of these slaves, a boy his own age named Allison. They met sometimes in a shop when Allison was sent to buy provisions for Master Nattie.

Allison's trousers and shirt were always ragged. He'd never been given a pair of shoes. He was, he often confessed to Peter, " 'most always hungry." Nat Gist worked his slaves far harder than Fisher had done. "When he's sober," said Allison, "he's maybe not much worse than other masters. Trouble is, he's 'most always drunk."

Peter learned this for himself during his first week with his new master. One evening Master Nattie came home so drunk he could hardly sit on his horse. As he dismounted, he threw the reins to Peter and ordered the boy to scatter a couple of bundles of oats on the ground for the horse.

Peter did so as his master staggered off toward the house. Suddenly, however, Nattie turned and came back to the yard. "What the devil did you throw the oats all about for?" he shouted at Peter.

"Why, Master," Peter said, "you told me to scatter them."

Gist raised his cane, brought it down hard on Peter's head. "I didn't tell you to scatter them all over the yard. Follow me to the house. I'll give you a lesson."

Peter walked slowly behind him to the door.

Gist's house looked fine enough on the outside. But inside, the front room contained only a few old pieces of furniture, some clothes which hung from nails in the bare wall—and the stench of whiskey.

"Take off your shirt and cross your hands," Gist ordered.

Peter did so, knowing what was in store. Allison had told him that Master Nattie's favorite form of punishment was "bucking."

Gist lashed the boy's hands together and drew them down over Peter's knees. He took a long, stout stick from the corner and thrust it under Peter's knees, thereby locking him into position—a position conveniently exposing his rump and bared back.

Gist then took up his cowhide whip.

*I will not cry out,* the boy said fiercely to himself. *I will not let him know that I feel pain.*

If he had cried out, Gist might not have heard him, so busy was he shouting curses at Peter.

Again and again the whip shot through the air, cracked down on Peter's bare flesh. Peter saw his own blood leaking onto the rough wooden planks of the floor. At the first few lashes, a protective shock of numbness seemed to cover his body. But then the pain exploded all over him. There was no more skin. No more bones. He was made of blazing pain, as though he had been thrown into the fiery oven of the brick kiln.

Finally, gasping with exertion, Gist threw the blood-reddened whip to the floor. "There, you black cuss," he cried. "I mean to make a good nigger of you, and there's no way to do it but by showing you who's master."

Peter's lips were clenched. He feared if he opened his mouth he would start to scream and to sob.

Gist removed the stick from beneath Peter's legs and unbound his hands. "Next time," he warned, "I'll leave you in the buck all day long."

*There won't be no next time,* Peter vowed to himself.

Nor was there.

Peter turned out to be Nat Gist's favorite. This meant that in addition to his brickyard duties, Peter was called upon to serve Gist in the house when the old man came home in the evenings.

Old man. In fact, Gist was not old. And he was strong, as Peter had seen during the bucking. But when he was drunk enough, and helpless, he seemed an old man. Peter often had to undress him, pull the stinking cotton night-gown over his master's head, carry him into the small bedroom, and tuck the covers around him.

Gist was undoubtedly grateful for all these ministrations. Yet he never uttered a word of appreciation or affection. He continued to curse at the boy ripely and roughly. But it was always Peter he bellowed for when he reached home after his hours at the pub.

One night Nattie Gist came home cursing, not at Peter but at two white men who had, it appeared, set up a Sabbath School for slaves. "Teaching niggers to read and write!" Gist emitted a shout of laughter at the ludicrous idea. Then he turned on Peter, his eyes narrowed with fury. "Any of *my* property goes near that school, and he'll get such a flogging he'll never need any more education or anything else. You understand me, boy?"

"Yes, Master," said Peter politely. "Would you like your hot coffee now?"

The following Sunday morning Peter appeared at the small clapboard church on the outskirts of town where, he had learned, the two white men had opened their school for slaves. The hope that had nearly faded during the years now swelled up again within him.

If he could learn to write, he could start to search for his family. He would write a letter to a Philadelphia newspaper. He would describe how he and his brother had been kidnaped by Mr. Kincaid. Surely his parents must have told the story to many people: how they came home one August afternoon to find their two small boys had disappeared. Maybe someone who had heard this story would read Peter's letter. And maybe then they would write to him. And he would read the letter. And he would know at last where his family was.

*Read*. And *write*. These were the keys he had been searching for. When he learned, he could unlock the doors to the past. He could find his home again, and his freedom.

His heart pounded heavily as he entered the church.

A scattering of black boys and men sat in the church pews. A white man was at the pulpit, but he was not preaching. He was holding up a big sign with three letters printed on it. And, like a chorus, the students chanted, "Cow."

"Correct," said the teacher, and pointed at each of the letters. "C–O–W. Cow." Then he lowered the card and looked at Peter. "Good morning," he said pleasantly. "You've come to join us?"

Peter nodded.

"Good," said the teacher. "What's your name?"

"Peter."

"Peter what?"

"Gist," he mumbled.

"Sorry," said the teacher, "I didn't hear you."

Peter mumbled the name again, even more indistinctly. Once the teacher found out that he was the slave of Nat Gist, Peter's career as a student would be ended.

"May I have your pass?" the teacher said.

Peter stared at him blankly.

"Every student must have a pass from his master," the teacher explained. "I can only teach students who come here with the written approval of their owners."

"My—my master didn't know that," Peter stammered. "But he don't mind that I come here. It was him who told me about this school."

The teacher nodded. "All right. Take a seat, Peter. But next Sunday be sure to have a written pass. Otherwise, I can't let you in."

That afternoon Peter raced into the cabin where his brother lay sleeping. He shook Levin's shoulder to wake him. "I can write my name!" he cried. "Look!" He took a stick and on the hard-packed earth of the floor drew five letters:

## PƎTƎꓤ

Then he stood up and announced to Levin, "That says *Peter*! This is me. Peter."

Levin was impressed. But when he learned about the need for a pass to attend next Sunday's school, Levin frowned. "You know Master Nattie will never give you no pass," he said. "He told you already he'll beat any nigger of his to death for going to that school."

"He's not going to beat me to death," Peter declared. "I'm his property. He's not going to kill his property."

"Maybe he won't kill you," said Levin. "But he'll beat you sure enough. Seems to me like it ain't worth a beating, just to scratch some little lines in the ground."

"Seems to you that way," said Peter, "so you stay home and sleep some more next Sunday. Me—I'm going back to school!"

And the following Sunday he did go back.

When the teacher asked for his pass, he said, "I—I forgot to ask. But Master was real glad I learned how to write my name. He said to tell you thank you. That he was real proud of me."

The teacher frowned a little. Then he said, "Who *is* your master, Peter?"

But Peter had already taken a seat in one of the pews and was talking busily to another boy.

The teacher shrugged and went on with the lesson.

When the class was over, however, he called Peter to him and said, "You're a bright boy, Peter. I like having you in my class. But I'm afraid I can't allow you in next Sunday unless you come with a written pass from your master."

Peter nodded a little. He stared at the floor.

"You see," said the teacher, "if we accept one single student without his master's permission, they can close the whole school. Mr. Gumperts and I had to fight hard enough to get this school opened in the first place. In some states anyone who teaches a Negro to read or write must pay a fine of $150 to $200. That's not the case in Lexington. But there is a lot of feeling roused up against our school. Mr. Gumperts and I have got to stick to our promise, Peter. We can't teach a student unless his master agrees to it."

"My—master agrees," said Peter in a low voice. "I told you, sir, he was the one who first let me know about this school."

"Well, then, be sure, son, to bring the pass next week."

No white man had ever spoken to him in this kind way. It made Peter's throat tighten.

When he left the church he walked slowly down the dusty dirt road, wondering what he should do. He didn't want to get the teacher in trouble. He didn't want the school to be closed because of him.

But—if he could just go there one more time, maybe if he tried very hard, he could learn enough so that he could write out the pass himself and pretend that it came from Nattie Gist!

The following Sunday morning he arrived late and waited by the doorway until the teacher had turned to write a word on a large card. Then he slid into a back row and sat very low in the seat, hoping he would not be seen.

"Peter," the teacher said quietly. "Your pass, please."

"My master, he's gone away. Gone down South for a spell. Before I got to see him, he was gone. Don't rightly know when he'll be back, sir."

"Well," said the teacher, "the school will still be here

43

when your master returns. So when you have your pass, come back, son. You'll be very welcome."

"Couldn't I stay just this *one* more time?" Peter cried. "Then I won't trouble you no more! I promise!"

"I'm afraid not," the teacher said slowly. "Or maybe you'll understand me better if I just say—I'm afraid."

Peter nodded. He stood up and walked slowly out the door.

On the way home he reflected that he had, after all, learned a few things. He could write his name and most of the alphabet. He could write the numbers 1 through 10. And he had learned that a white man could be kind.

When Peter was seventeen, he was hired out in the winter to a tobacconist named George Norton.

Norton owned a fine-looking shop in Lexington. And he was a fine-looking man. He always wore a broad-brimmed hat, and his hair descended behind in a stiff queue. The very smoke from his cigar seemed to rise in a pompous manner. He used his cane, which was his constant companion, to accent his various moods. He would tap it gently on the floor as he conversed genially with a customer. But should a slave displease him, the cane would slash through the air, a vicious weapon.

Norton rarely struck his workers, however, for the simple reason that they were not *his* slaves. He rented them all, with the exception of his body-servant, named Albert. When he wished to vent his anger by lashing one of the rented slaves, he often took it out instead on Albert.

One afternoon as Peter and several other slaves watched in horror, Albert was put in a buck and Norton lashed his naked back three hundred times with a cowhide. Blood gushed out and ran in streams onto the brick floor of the shop.

When Norton removed the stick from behind the slave's knees, Albert was unable to rise. This sent the tobacconist into another fit of rage. Norton seized a board full of shingle nails and struck Albert several violent blows. Each blow brought more blood, which jetted out in small spurts.

The other slaves stood paralyzed with fear. But Peter could not contain his revulsion and rage. "That man never going to strip me and put me in a buck to whip me," he declared under his breath, speaking to no one in particular. "I would die first."

He had not intended for Norton to overhear his words. But just as the tobacconist was going out the door, he turned suddenly and stared hard at Peter. He said nothing, however, and after a moment he abruptly left the shop.

The next Saturday evening as Peter was sweeping the floor, an old beggar woman came in and asked for some tobacco. Peter gathered up a handful of the sweepings and gave them to her.

He spent Sunday, as usual, at Master Nattie's. He played marbles. He slept. And he showed off the new blue linsey suit that Nattie Gist had bought for him. At seventeen, Peter was a strong, fine-looking boy. But he had never before *felt* good-looking—not until he paraded in his blue linsey suit, the first real suit he had ever owned.

On Monday morning he was wearing the suit when he came to work at Norton's shop. The tobacconist stood in the doorway. His eyes looked darker and brighter than usual, and the smoke from his cigar came in quick puffs. His cane beat an ominous march on the floor.

"Whose business was it to make a fire in the sweat-room yesterday?" The words shot out at Peter.

"Mine, sir," said Peter.

"Did you attend to it?"

"Yes, sir."

"And then?"

"It was Sunday, sir. So I went up home to Master Nattie's."

"I'll let you know, nigger," George Norton bellowed, "*this* is your home. And *I* am your master."

"Yes, sir," Peter said. It was an unspoken rule in Norton's shop that a slave should call no other man "master." Though he owned none of the slaves but Albert, he liked to pretend to himself that he was the master of all of them.

The harsh tapping of Norton's cane on the floor increased in tempo. "Who gave tobacco to an old woman on Saturday night?"

"I gave her a handful of sweepings, sir—no 'count, nohow, sir."

"I am your master," Norton thundered. "You are to obey me. Lie down across that box."

Peter did so. Was the man going to beat him? Every slave Peter had ever seen whipped was first asked to take off his shirt. No master wanted to destroy clothes, which he would have to replace. But then, Nattie Gist, not Norton, had bought Peter this fine blue linsey suit.

Norton took up a switch and struck Peter a violent blow.

Peter raised up, in pain and wrath.

"Lie down, you nigger," Norton screamed. And struck again.

Once more Peter rose up. And once more Norton's switch lashed at him, along with words. "Lie down, I said!"

For the third time Peter lay flat across the box. The switch fell with force, cutting his neck and slashing through his suit. "You cursed nigger," Norton shouted. "If you move once more before I am finished, I will beat you till you cannot rise."

Peter stood up. He looked at Norton steadily and said, "I have laid down three times for you to beat me, when I have done nothing wrong. I will not lie down again."

For a moment Norton stared at him, astounded. Then he seized Peter and tried to force the slave down across the box. But he could not do so. Whereupon he called out, "Mr. Kisich! Tadlock! All of you! Help me conquer this nigger!"

The overseer, Mr. Kisich, and three other white men who worked in the shop all fell upon Peter at once. They tried to tie his hands, but he struggled so fiercely that they did not succeed. They managed to throw him on the floor, but he screamed and struggled and bit their legs and ankles. It was clear that they could not hold him down unless they could tie him. They got a rope, but he writhed and kicked with his arms and legs. They made a noose of the rope and put it over his head. Peter quickly raised both hands, thrust them through the noose, and slipped it down below his arms, thus thwarting their intention of choking him.

With the rope fastened around his waist, the men dragged him to the back of the shop where there were five heavy tobacco presses, each eight feet high. They tried to hang him up on one of these, but as they raised the rope to fasten it to the top of the press, Peter sprang to one side and crept into the narrow space between the press and the wall.

There he remained, bleeding, panting, glaring at his tormentors, who stood on either side of the press, beating him over the head with cowhides and hoop-poles, thrusting sticks and pieces of iron against his bleeding body.

They kept this up for two hours, until Peter had no more strength to resist and they were able to drag him out. Norton threw him across a keg and whipped him with a cowhide, swearing all the while that this was the first nigger who had ever tried to fight him, and that Peter would be humbled if it took his life.

When Norton had finished, it was nearly ten o'clock in the morning. He looked at the other slaves, who stood watching helplessly, and ordered them to go to work. Then Norton, his overseer, and the other three white men went to the main house for breakfast. "With all that exercise," said the overseer, "I've worked up quite an appetite." And he laughed loudly.

Peter, nearly naked, his new suit cut to shreds, crept out of the shop. Staggering, sometimes crawling, he managed to make his way up the hill to his master's house.

Gist was not there. But Aunt Mary, the cook, dressed Peter's wounds and then helped him back to the slave quarters. She brought her own blanket to put over the straw that was his bed and mattress. And when he lay feverish and groaning with pain Aunt Mary said, "Let us hope you have learned yourself a lifetime lesson."

"What lesson?" Peter said.

She looked down at him, astonished. "Why—never to talk back to no white man!"

Peter said nothing. But when she had left and he lay alone in the empty cabin, he answered her. "I learned my lesson, Aunt Mary. I learned I got to find some way to get back home. To be free."

# 7

The following week he found a way.

Nattie Gist had allowed Peter to remain at home for a week until his wounds healed and his strength returned. This was no great act of kindness on Gist's part, for Peter was scarcely able to sit up, much less go to work. Furthermore, since the tobacconist had inflicted damage on the property of Nattie Gist, it was only right, Gist insisted, that George Norton continue to pay him while said property recovered.

Peter was lonely in the cabin, and Aunt Mary came in when she could to keep him company. She was a gossipy woman who regaled him with tales, some of them fantasy, some of them true.

One afternoon she sat down by his bed with a story so terrible it could only be true.

It concerned a slave named Spencer, whose master, a Mr. Williams, owned a lottery office in Lexington.

"I seen that Spencer myself," said Aunt Mary. "A fine-looking mulatto. A fine-looking man."

Mr. Williams, she said, often hired Spencer out to livery stables or to hotels, where he worked as a waiter. Williams, of course, received the money for Spencer's services. But if the slave worked on Sundays and in the evenings, Spencer was allowed to keep the money he made.

"He made money," said Peter slowly, "and he—he could *keep* it?"

Aunt Mary nodded, pleased at Peter's show of interest. "He was good at doctoring horses. He got good pay for this and kept the money he got. Now, what do you think he was saving it up for? What do you suppose he wanted to buy?"

"Don't know," said Peter.

"Himself!" she exclaimed.

Peter frowned, puzzled.

Aunt Mary laughed. "That's what I said, boy. This Spencer, he asked his master what kind of price Mr. Williams would sell him for. 'Don't rightly know,' says Mr. Williams. 'I expect around a thousand dollars.' So Spencer up and asks, 'Would you sell me—to *me* for a thousand dollars?' Williams looks at him. Then he busts out laughing and says, 'Well, sure I will!' "

Peter's heart started to pound. *This* was the way! This was what he'd been searching for. He had thought often of running away. But where would he run to? With no money? No one to help him? The Lexington jail was, he knew, always crowded with runaway slaves. Ever since he was nine years old he'd heard horror stories of the bloodhounds and the men with guns who set out to capture runaway slaves. There seemed to be no chance at all of running away successfully and becoming free.

But if a man could *buy* himself—buy his freedom!

"What happened?" he asked, his eagerness to know nearing desperation.

"What happened?" Aunt Mary shook her head with somber wisdom. "What happened was that as Spencer made his own money he turned it over to his master. Every cent of it. Every dollar. Finally—after four years—he had earned $975. He worked every Sunday and every night doctoring horses, sweeping out stables, working in the Phoenix Hotel restaurant and kitchen. And when he had earned $975, and had only $25 more to go, why then—" She paused.

"*What?*" Peter exclaimed.

"Why then," said Aunt Mary, "this white man, Mr. Williams, says he had never promised that Spencer could buy himself! And he was *keeping* Spencer's money, for a slave's earnings belong to his master. And Spencer, he says, must never raise the matter again."

Peter nodded, crushed.

"*But*," Aunt Mary continued, "Spencer did not give up hope."

"No?" said Peter, his own hope stirring again. Perhaps Spencer had found a white man he could trust. Perhaps he *had* bought his freedom.

"Another gentleman heard the story," said Aunt Mary. "He came to Spencer and said it was an outrage. That was the word he used—an outrage. He said that if Spencer earned *another* thousand dollars, and paid it to *him*, this gentleman would then buy Spencer from Mr. Williams— and give him his freedom.

"So Spencer set himself out to earn another thousand dollars. But this time, he played it smart. When he made a payment he asked for a written receipt from the gentleman. And finally, after four more years, when he had earned all but seventy of that thousand dollars—" Once again she paused dramatically.

"What happened?" Peter burst out.

She laughed, but the sound was sour. "The white man left town, and no one never heard from him again."

"No!" Peter cried out. "That can't be true!"

"The story's not finished," said Aunt Mary. "Spencer brung out all his receipts. But they was all a trick! They didn't even show the name of the man who had taken his money. And then Spencer was sold to a new master. And would you believe—" She laughed shrilly. "That fool Spencer asked to buy freedom from *him*—for a thousand dollars!"

"The third time!" Peter cried in anguish.

Aunt Mary nodded. "This time he earned the full thousand dollars. And when he went to his master for his free papers and a pass out of the state—what do you s'pose happened?"

Peter could only stare at her, unable to answer and afraid to hear.

"It happened just yesterday," said Aunt Mary. "I heard about it when I went down to the dry-goods store this morning. Instead of getting his free papers and a pass, Spencer was chained in a gang and sent off to the Deep South!"

Peter lay back, horrified, defeated.

Yet long after Aunt Mary had gone, he kept thinking about the idea. Perhaps somewhere . . . somehow . . . someday he would find a white man who was honest. . . . A man who would give him the chance to earn his own money and—buy himself!

Anyway, it was something to hang a hope on.

In the winter of 1818 Nattie Gist died.

Peter and Levin were willed to Gist's nephew, Levi, along with "one plain cherry bedstead with bedding ($18), bowl and pitcher ($3), one sorrel horse ($50), Aunt Mary ($750); 10 sacks of coffee at 9 cents lb.; and one barrel of sperm oil, $1.30."

Aunt Mary, despite all her advice to Peter, promptly forgot everything she had told him. When she found she had been "willed away" from Kentucky, she became hysterical with grief. She knew and liked Master Levi. He would be a far kinder owner than Nattie Gist had been. But Master Levi lived in the Deep South, in a place called Bainbridge, Alabama. And moving to Alabama would mean leaving her husband, Sam.

Sam was a native African, who still spoke broken English. He was a powerful, handsome man who had declared to his importer that if he were not set free in ten years' time, he would kill himself. So the contract had been drawn; and now Sam's day of freedom was drawing close.

Aunt Mary had expected that all her years of devoted service as cook and house servant for Nattie Gist would be rewarded with *her* freedom when her master died. Now, instead, she was to be passed on with the cherry bedstead in which Master Nattie had died.

But Mary refused. She would not leave Lexington and her husband, Sam. They might kill her, she said, but she would not go. Indeed, she would hang herself first.

Levi Gist tried his best to persuade her to come to Alabama, but she was adamant. He therefore sold Aunt Mary to his father, who lived in Lexington, so that she could remain with Sam.

Peter took note of all these proceedings and considered making the same dire threats. But he knew that Mary was prepared to carry out her words and *would* hang herself if she were forced to leave Kentucky. Peter, however, fully intended to live out his life. He also knew that Levi Gist would never believe him should he threaten suicide. The outcome of such a threat would no doubt be delivery to a slave trader. And, although Peter had no wish to leave Lexington and dreaded living in the Deep South, at least he and Levin would be together, in Alabama; and Levi Gist was known to be a good master.

Indeed, there was even the faint hope that Levi Gist might be the man who would allow Peter to buy his own freedom.

# 8

On a cold Sunday morning five days before Christmas, in the year 1818, Peter and Master John Gist, the younger brother of Levi, left Lexington on horseback. Levin had departed earlier with Levi Gist.

The trip to Bainbridge, John Gist said, took eighteen days if the going was good. And the going *was* good.

Peter and John were about the same age, and John Gist treated Peter like a friend, not a slave. They sang and talked together as their horses trotted, cantered, walked along the country roads. In the evenings they stopped at inns or hotels. Master John would adjourn to the parlor, where he sat by a blazing fire telling the news from Lexington. And Peter would repair to the kitchen, where he became the center of attention as he described the fine city in which he had lived: a city that boasted a public library, a museum, two newspapers, a college, beautiful parks, fine hotels, a stately courthouse, a theater, a coffee house, a Gentlemen's Club, Sam Brown's Lexington Medical Society, which was housed in a large brick building, and streets of shops that sold such luxury items as Spanish "seegars," paisley shawls, imported china, and silver bowls. Indeed, as Peter took pains to point out, Lexington silversmiths were famous the country over. He would also talk about Ashland and Senator Clay, who had by now become one of the most noted figures in national politics.

Peter found that he loved an audience. He would often keep talking until two or three in the morning, quite forgetting that he and John Gist had to ride on the next day.

Since neither young man was in any hurry to arrive at Bainbridge, John, too, would frequently retire late and rise around noon.

With good companionship, a good horse, fine food at the inns, excellent weather, ever-changing and ever-new territories and towns to ride through, and the rapt attention Peter received from new listeners in the evenings, the trip turned out to be the first vacation he had ever known. He enjoyed himself hugely, and for the first time he felt what it would be like to be free.

However, when they reached the northwest corner of Tennessee, not far from Bainbridge, worries began to set in.

The region looked bleak, almost menacing. The brown, desolate fields were covered with frosted cotton shrubs. The huge trees by the roadside were leafless, grim, and cast gloomy, skeletal shadows. Swollen rivulets rushed angrily along to the nearby Tennessee River.

Peter and John had forded many streams and rivers on their way South. And each time they regarded it as an adventure, even when their horses balked midstream and the two young men had to dismount and lead them through the icy waters.

But as they neared their destination, the swollen streams seemed suddenly frightening to Peter. His horse perhaps sensed his fear and, for the first time, bucked and reared and refused to enter the water.

What Peter found most depressing of all was the people they passed. In Kentucky he had been used to seeing the miserable shanties in which slaves lived. But here, white folks, too, lived in hovels. Their clothing was as wretched as that of any slave he had ever seen. Indeed, it was worse, for in the wintertime most slaves were given shoes. Here children, women, and even men were barefoot.

Nor had he ever seen children like these: white-haired, sallow-skinned, scrawny, bone-thin. They did not respond to a greeting, but stared sullenly as the two riders went by.

By the time they rode into the town of Bainbridge, Alabama, a feeling of dread had settled inside Peter. The Deep South looked far worse than anything he had ever imagined.

Where were the fine plantation homes he had seen earlier on their trip South? He had imagined himself working as a servant in Master Levi's home: a trusted servant learning to read and write, making money on the side, and buying his way to freedom.

But the town of Bainbridge consisted of some thirty small log cabins scattered here and there among tall forest trees, most of which were dead.

"Well, Peter," said John cheerily, "how do you like the looks of the place?"

After a moment Peter replied, as politely as he could, "Doesn't look like a town, Master John. I never knew folks to have a town in the *woods*."

"Oh, the woods will be gone in a few years," said John. "Don't you see that many of these trees are dead now? They girdle them, and the next year the trees die and are chopped down."

Peter looked at the tree trunks that were slashed deep with ax wounds to prevent the sap from running, so that the trees would slowly die.

"Where's the store?" he asked then. "You told me Master Levi has a store here in Bainbridge."

John pointed. "There. Where that gentleman is sitting on the porch."

"That the *store!*" Peter exclaimed. "Don't look any bigger than a kitchen!" Then he asked, almost afraid to hear the answer, "Where does Master Levi—live?"

"Right here!" said John. He jumped off his horse and gave the reins to Peter, who stared straight ahead: there were two small log cabins with an open passage between them.

John ran up the porch steps and into the house. Peter sat on his horse, staring.

"*This* is where Master Levi *lives!*" He spoke the words out loud, though there was no one to hear him. He remembered old Master Nattie's voice crowing with glee as he described the wealth of his nephews in Alabama. "What would Master Nattie say if he could see his young gentlemen living in a cabin in the woods among poor white folks?"

He answered his own question. "Master Nattie, you would whirl in your grave!"

Nevertheless, for two weeks the hope by which Peter lived was able to survive, even to grow.

He was not sent to the cotton fields. Master Levi told him to help Aunt Peggy with the cooking and to "get acquainted with the town."

Getting acquainted did not take long in this town of thirty log cabins and a general store. Peter centered his hopes in the store, for it was owned by the Gist brothers. It contained not only the assortment of dry goods and groceries with which country stores are usually supplied, but also a stock of rum, whiskey, and even imported liquors. Furthermore, it contained the Bainbridge Post

Office. With these inducements to congregate, the Gist General Store was the social hub of Bainbridge. From early morning till late at night, men gathered in the store and on its front porch, talking, arguing, laughing lustily, sometimes brawling. It was Peter's firm hope that he would be sent to work in the store. Here he would come to know every man and woman in town. Here he might find the white man whom he could trust with his plan.

Peter also learned that during the winter months slaves had some chance to earn their own pocket money. Flatboats that came down the river loaded with cotton were frequently caught on rocks in the Muscle Shoals, just above Bainbridge. River water seeped into the cotton, which was then useless for market, unless the bales were opened and the cotton dried. Every Sunday, therefore—except when it rained—slaves gathered at the river's edge. They spent the day spreading damp cotton on boards or boulders in the sunshine, turning and shaking it till it was perfectly dry and fit to be packed once again in bales for market. For this the slaves sometimes received as much as a dollar a day.

How many years would it take to make a thousand Sundays? How old would Peter be by the time he had saved enough to buy his freedom? He could only wish that he had been permitted to spend more time in the church school. Then he might have learned enough to be able to figure out such problems.

At the end of January, Levi Gist announced that Peter had now been given sufficient time to get acquainted with the town. He would henceforth work in the cotton fields.

The only bright part of the dismal first day was that he and Levin were reunited. Together they worked their way up and down the winter fields with freedom to talk about the future, which looked bleak, and the distant past, which was now so far away it was almost forgotten.

Then, as they plucked cotton from the frost-browed bolls, Levin revealed to Peter that he had something of interest to report about the present: he had found a woman he loved and wanted to marry. Her name was Fanny. She was, said Levin with a soft smile, "a pretty little thing. She's a good girl, too," he added after a moment. "Even though she does belong to old Jimmy Hogun."

During his two weeks of getting acquainted, Peter had heard much about this Jimmy Hogun, whose place was known throughout the countryside. Hogun was a bachelor. He boasted that no white woman had ever set foot in his house. But there were many females who lived on the premises, all of them beautiful young slave girls. And, Peter had learned, "patrollers and other wild and reckless characters" gathered there every night. Hogun supplied his girls and his whiskey, for a price.

Peter set down his bag of cotton and stared at his brother. "What you want with one of *those* girls?" he asked.

"But my Fanny ain't one of those girls," Levin insisted. "She's the daughter of Aunt Linsey, old Jimmy Hogun's housekeeper. Fanny works in the kitchen, out of the way of those wild men. She's a good girl."

Peter nodded a little, unconvinced. He continued picking cotton in silence.

Levin laughed a little, a bitter sound. "You talk the same as Master Levi!"

"Well, maybe Master Levi got good sense," said Peter grimly.

"He got no sense at all!" Levin burst out. "I told him I want to marry. And Master Levi says fine, I can get me a wife soon as I wish, so long as she is the right sort. But when I tell him who I want to marry, he flies in a rage. 'No boy of mine shall be spending his nights and Sundays at old Jimmy Hogun's,' he says. 'So don't talk no more to me about it. Hunt up another girl. Or I'll find someone for you. But don't talk no more to me about a girl from Jimmy Hogun's place!' "

"So—what you going to do?" Peter asked.

"Do?" said Levin. "I'm going to marry my Fanny. She is the woman I want. And she is the woman I'm going to have for my wife. And no other!"

At the end of that day, when the slaves brought their bags to Master Andrew Gist to be weighed, it was found that Peter had picked less than anyone, even the young girls. A mere twelve and a half pounds! The others, highly amused, gathered around him, taunting and laughing.

Master Andrew said nothing about it to Peter. But he put forth a surprising announcement. If any slave could pick fifty pounds of cotton the next day, he would be given a prize: a new pair of shoes.

There was much excitement about this prize, though no one expected to win it. Fifty pounds was a heap of cotton for one man to pick in a day.

Peter barely spoke the next day; he moved through the rows swiftly, his long, nimble fingers in constant motion, plucking the soft, fleecy cotton from the bolls. And by evening, to everyone's surprise, his bags weighed in at seventy-five pounds.

After this, he was seldom surpassed in the cotton fields. But he often wondered what his hard work was achieving. Why would the Gist brothers take a man who was doing so well for them in the fields and let him work in the store? And Peter's immediate goal in life was to escape from the grinding, boring work in the cotton fields to the only place in Bainbridge where the varied pulse of life was felt: the Gist General Store.

Two years later, Levi Gist built himself a new brick house in Bainbridge. The lower story was turned over to the new General Store. He also bought a plantation of four hundred and eighty acres, which lay seven miles south of his home. Then, to crown his achievements, he brought home a beautiful young bride.

She was from Nashville. Her name, before she became Mrs. Gist, had been Miss Thirmuthis Waters. She was the sister of Mrs. McKiernan, and it was on the McKiernan plantation that Levi and Thirmuthis Waters had met and fallen in love.

Levi promised Thirmuthis that she could have her pick of any of his slaves as her house servant. She went out to the cotton fields and spent time speaking to each one. She selected Peter.

He adored his new mistress. She was not only beautiful, but generous, cheerful, and even-tempered. He had heard many tales of sweet, gentle mistresses so delicate they would shiver in an unexpected draft of evening air; yet these same ladies, thinking nothing of the feat, could strip and tie their slaves, both men and women, and beat them with the zest of a burly overseer. Indeed, Miss 'Muthis's sister, Mrs. McKiernan, was said to be one of these fearsome women. But Peter's mistress rarely even raised her voice in displeasure. Nor did Peter give her cause to do so.

He was, for the first time, happy in his work. He served as cook, servant, and waiter. There was no other slave in the house except a small boy named Teddy, who was brought in to help Peter in his many duties.

What cheered Peter the most was the fact that he had finally found someone who would help him. He had now saved almost $50, most of it earned by drying cotton at the riverbanks on Sundays. Fifty dollars was a long way from a thousand. But at least it was a start. And Miss 'Muthis could certainly persuade Levi Gist to accept Peter's money and allow him to buy himself!

Then, one Sunday evening in early spring, there occurred a shattering event. It convinced Peter his mistress might not have the power he hoped she had, when it came to convincing her husband about a matter concerning slaves.

Levin had walked the seven miles from the plantation to Bainbridge. He had something special to tell Peter—and Levi Gist. He had married Fanny Hogun. He felt that Master Levi would understand now, since the master himself was so happy in marriage.

Levin stood before his master and mistress, shamefaced, trying to explain. "I tried not to love her, sir. But I couldn't help it. There was no other woman in the world that I wanted for my wife. Only Fanny. So—we're married, sir. And I come to ask you, can I visit her on Sundays?"

Peter was standing in the doorway watching, and waiting for Levi Gist's reply. But Master Levi simply stared wordlessly at Levin.

Thirmuthis touched her husband's arm. "I'm sure Fanny *is* a good girl," she said softly. "Even though she was brought up in that place."

Levi Gist seemed not to have heard his wife's words. He went into the bedroom and returned with a rope and a cowhide whip.

"No!" Thirmuthis begged. "Don't! Please!"

Levi Gist said nothing at all. He bound Levin, who stood as if turned to stone. Then Gist took up his whip and started to count as each separate lash brought a new streak of blood to Levin's scarred back.

At first Levin made no outcry. But the lashing went on and on. . . . Thirty strokes. . . . Fifty. . . . Ninety. . . . Then he started to scream, cry, and plead with his master to stop.

"For God's sake, sir!" Peter burst out. "Stop beating my brother!" He grabbed his master's arm, but Gist knocked him to the floor and shouted, "Leave off, nigger, or you'll get the same!"

Thirmuthis ran from the room.

And the whipping went on.

Three hundred and seventeen lashes fell upon Levin's bleeding back, which by now had sections of skin hanging from it. Levin lay on the floor, whimpering. Peter tried to raise him up, but Levin screamed in pain.

Suddenly Peter's anger exploded. "Look what you have done!" he shouted at his master. "Look what you have done to my brother!"

Levi Gist stared through Peter as though he had not spoken, as though he were not even there in the room. Gist gazed down at the man on the floor, the man he had lashed three hundred and seventeen times. Carefully he hung the bloody whip behind the door and walked slowly from the room.

The following evening as Peter was preparing dinner, Levi Gist entered the kitchen. For a long moment he said nothing. Peter continued slicing sugar beets, unable to look at his master.

Finally, Gist said, "I—I would like you to tell your brother that I'm sorry. I did him a grievous wrong. I acted too hastily, in a passion. And I am very sorry."

Peter nodded a little. But he did not speak. He could not.

"You may tell your brother," said Levi Gist, "that he is free to visit his wife every Sunday. And I will tell my overseer that Fanny may come to visit Levin whenever she is able to do so."

Peter knew he should thank his master, but the words stuck in his throat. He merely nodded again.

As though the matter were ended forever, Levi Gist said, "I see we're having beets for dinner. Never did care much for sugar beets." And he laughed, just a little.

# 9

Peter tried to forget the brutal lashing his brother had received for the crime of marrying the girl he loved. He knew that if he could not drive the scene from his mind, he could no longer work as house servant for Levi Gist. At the age of twenty-one, Peter had a position envied by every one of Gist's slaves. And Master Levi, he realized, would never keep him in the house were he to show the bitterness he felt.

So he resumed the outward pleasantness he had always displayed. But his hope of one day being able to buy his freedom from his master was dead.

What frightened him most was the fact that Levi Gist was considered to be the kindest slave-owner in the county. If Peter were ever sold, it seemed to him almost certain that the new owner would be far worse. He might even be a man like McKiernan, Levi Gist's brother-in-law. McKiernan's slaves were said to be the worst fed, the worst clothed, the worst housed, the worst treated of any in the Bainbridge area.

The following year Peter had much opportunity to observe the truth of McKiernan's grim reputation.

Levi Gist had sold his interest in the Bainbridge store to his brother. Levi then moved his family to the plantation, where, he declared, he would henceforth devote his attentions to "hunting and to agricultural pursuits." However, he tended to leave the agricultural pursuits to his overseer, and took off with his hounds at the dawn of every day for the sport he most loved.

This meant that his wife had little company, and less to do. The "great house" to which Levi had brought her consisted of two cabins built of hewn logs, whitewashed inside and out with lime. A covered passage connected the rooms, over each of which was a small, low chamber. Outside were a log kitchen, a smokehouse, and several other small shed-like buildings, a washhouse, a spinning house, a toolshed, a stable. This completed Mistress Gist's domain. And since Peter and several other slaves were there to see that she need not lift a finger to do any sort of work whatever, Thirmuthis grew bored.

She began to spend more and more time at the nearby McKiernan plantation visiting with her older sister, Letitia, McKiernan's wife. Since she always chose Peter to drive her there and back, he found himself, for the first time, something of a man of leisure. Many of his afternoon hours were spent merely waiting around till Miss 'Muthis was ready to be driven home again. Peter, used to working hard since the age of nine, found this new situation rather unsettling—until the afternoon when he met McKiernan's newest purchase, a slender, shy young slave girl named Lavinia, though everyone called her Vina.

She had been sold by her owner at an hour's notice, to pay off gambling debts. And she had been taken from her home in Lawrence County, Alabama, before she even had time to say good-by to her mother and brothers.

Peter chanced to be in the room when Vina was first interviewed by her new master and mistress. He would often ask for things to do to occupy his time, and on this afternoon had been given some silver to polish. He looked up as Vina was shown into the room, and when she glanced at him he nodded and smiled a little, trying to give her some encouragement, for the girl was obviously terrified.

Mrs. McKiernan, a handsome, imposing lady, had a voice that could be demure when speaking to her husband. But she generally spoke harshly when addressing a slave.

"What can you do, girl?" she inquired of Vina.

Vina answered so softly that she could not be heard.

"Speak up, girl!" Mrs. McKiernan's words were sharp as a slap.

"I've been used to nursing, ma'am, and waiting in the house."

"Did you never work in the field, girl?"

"No, ma'am."

"Ah! You've been raised quite a lady! Can you weed corn?"

"I—I don't know, ma'am."

"Can you thin cotton?"

"No, ma'am."

"You're such a lady, I suppose you never saw any cotton grow."

"Yes, ma'am, I seen a plenty of cotton growing, but I never worked it."

At this point Mr. McKiernan walked up to the girl. Without saying a word, he turned her around, unfastened her frock, shoved it off her shoulders, and examined her back. "Have you ever been whipped?"

"No, sir."

"So I thought. Your back is as smooth as mine."

Then, as Vina stood before him naked from the waist up, McKiernan proceeded to make a careful inspection, running his hands over her body, her arms, her legs. As an afterthought he opened the girl's mouth and looked at her teeth.

Watching this, Peter felt rage swell within him; and he felt Vina's agonizing shame.

The master and mistress then discussed their new possession as Vina pulled up her frock and fastened it again. It was decided that she should serve as housemaid and wait on table, and that Martha, who had held this post, would be sent out to the cotton fields.

In most households, Peter knew, the post of house servant would be regarded as a prized one. But Mrs. McKiernan was known for her ready use of the whip. Only the day before she had lashed Martha so severely that the girl could not button her dress and went about with her raw-welted back exposed.

Perhaps Mr. McKiernan had somewhat the same thought as Peter, for, as Vina left the room, he said to his wife: "Let us hope that her back can remain as smooth as it is now—for a few months, at least."

And Mrs. McKiernan answered her husband sweetly, "If she follows instructions, she need have no fear."

Vina did follow instructions. The sight of Martha's scarred back was incentive enough. The girl was quick, careful, attentive, and for three months she managed to get by with barely a harsh word from her mistress.

During those same three months Peter found himself looking forward with ever more eagerness to the days on which he drove Miss 'Muthis to the McKiernan plantation.

There were many girls on Levi Gist's plantation, and in Bainbridge, who had made no secret of the fact that they wanted to marry Peter. He was handsome and well-built, though not tall. He was only 5 feet, 7 inches, but he walked tall, and there was an impressive air about him. He was intelligent, kind, strong-willed, intense; yet he knew well how to relax and to laugh. He also had somehow found the secret of how to get on with white people without humbling himself.

Peter, however, had always shrugged aside the matter of marriage. He revealed his reasons only to one person, Levin. Despite the ever more apparent impossibilities of the plan, he still hoped one day to buy his own freedom. He now had nearly $200 saved. He kept his money buried in a box below the wooden floor of the toolshed. If he did one day find a white man he could trust to help him, he certainly did not plan to be further tied to slavery by a wife and children.

But after three months of knowing Vina, he found that despite himself he was beginning to think about marriage.

At first he had spent what time he could with her, chiefly to cheer her. Though the girl was sweet and pleasant when serving her master and mistress, she was obviously only play-acting. When she left them she gave in to her own private sadness. Peter tried to wean her away from her sorrow. He found that it helped her to talk about her mother and her brothers, Jerry and Quall. The fact that she had been taken from them without even a chance to say goodby reminded Peter of his own tragedy, and brought back the raw fear and despair he had thought were long forgotten. His own experiences helped him to help Vina out of her misery, and he soon began to feel for her in ways that exceeded sympathy.

It also became very clear that Vina loved him and wanted to be his wife.

For a time, in order to avoid entanglement, Peter asked his mistress whether someone else might drive her to the McKiernan plantation. When she asked why, he confessed that one of McKiernan's slave girls kept bothering him about getting married. In fact, Vina had never said a word about marriage. But she did keep "bothering" him. And when he stopped seeing her, it was just as difficult as when he did see her. He thought about her through the days, and dreamed about her in the nights.

Finally, it seemed that he just had to see her again. Perhaps, after all, she would not be as beautiful as he remembered her—or as sweet, intelligent, sensitive, loving. . . .

Perhaps seeing her would help him to forget about her.

So he told Miss 'Muthis that the situation with McKiernan's slave girl had now righted itself. And he was prepared to drive his mistress to the plantation again.

Miss 'Muthis gave him a long, steady look and said quite seriously, "Are you sure, Peter? It's no trouble for me to find someone else as a driver. But there *would* be trouble—a lot of it—if you ever decided to marry one of McKiernan's slaves. You know that we're waiting for you to marry—at home."

"Yes, Missus," Peter said. Often enough she and the master had encouraged him to wed Bessie, or Sally, or Lula—healthy, young, and good-looking girls owned by Levi Gist. Peter well understood the economics of slavery. If he married one of McKiernan's girls, his child would belong to McKiernan. However—if McKiernan would sell Vina to Levi Gist . . . .

Peter dwelt on this possibility as he and his mistress drove toward the plantation. Then he caught his thoughts up sharp, as if he were drawing up the reins on a galloping horse. Here he was on his way to assure himself that he had built this girl up in his imaginings; that he did not, after all, love her. And he was, at the same time, planning how things could be worked out so that he *could* marry her.

He waited for her in the kitchen. She was, the cook told

him, in the Great House, serving lunch. He found to his dismay that his heart pounded at the very thought of seeing her again.

When at last she came through the door, a rush of emotions went through him. As for Vina, she stopped short upon seeing him and uttered a soft cry.

The cook, Aunt Hattie, muttered something about going out to the smokehouse, and left diplomatically.

Peter and Vina were alone.

"Where you—been all this time?" she asked finally.

"I been trying to stay away from you," Peter said, walking slowly toward her.

"Why you been trying that?"

He took her into his arms. For the first time, they kissed.

Presently Vina whispered, "I—I feel all strange. I got to sit down."

Peter lifted her in his arms. He sat in the kitchen chair, holding Vina on his lap. "That better?" he asked, and kissed her again.

Then she laughed a little. "This ain't no better," she said. "It's worse, much worse. But it's a nice kind of worse."

"I was hoping," Peter told her, "that seeing you would make me stop loving you. But it doesn't seem to be working out that way at all."

"Why you so set on not loving me?" Vina asked.

"Because Master Levi—he's set on me marrying one of his girls."

As soon as he had said them, he wished the words back in his mouth. Here he had come to rid himself of Vina, and he was talking about marrying her! It seemed he had two selves inside him. One he had known since early childhood: the self determined to keep free so that one day, he could *be* free.

72

And here was this new self undermining all his plans, getting him entangled for life with a girl . . . a girl he wanted for his wife . . . a girl he wanted as the mother of his children. A girl who would pull him deeply and irrevocably into the mire of slavery.

"Can Master Levi *make* you marry one of his girls?" Vina inquired.

"Never had no luck in that so far," Peter said.

She smiled softly, and once again they kissed—to be interrupted abruptly by the sharp voice of Mrs. McKiernan. "This is what you're doing, girl, while we're waiting in the house for our coffee!"

Vina fairly sprang off Peter's lap. "Sorry, Missus," she exclaimed. "I—I—" Overcome with confusion, she could say no more.

" 'T wasn't her fault, ma'am," said Peter earnestly, fearful that the scene might result in a lashing for Vina.

Surprisingly, Mrs. McKiernan merely laughed. "I'll keep your secret," she said. Then she went to the door. But before departing, she turned and said, "If you two should want to get married, I assure you Mr. McKiernan and I would be only too pleased." Then she smiled at Vina. "And now, girl, if you can bestir yourself to bring us our coffee . . . ."

"Yes, Missus, right away," Vina said.

Mrs. McKiernan left. And Vina turned to Peter, astounded. "All of a sudden she turned so—so nice!"

Peter nodded but said nothing. He knew full well why Mrs. McKiernan had turned so nice! And he knew that now there would be little hope of McKiernan selling Vina to Levi Gist. Why get rid of a girl who might soon produce some fine slave children for McKiernan to own, free of charge?

# 10

Events happened just as Peter had feared.

After that first reunion with Vina he knew that, despite all his hopes, dreams, plans for the faraway future, it was the present that mattered most. He was in love with the beautiful girl named Vina. She loved him. And they wanted to marry.

He mentioned the matter first to the only white person he had ever met whom he trusted completely, his mistress. He suggested that perhaps Master Levi might be willing to buy the girl. Mrs. Gist knew and liked Vina and she promised Peter that she would do her best to persuade her husband to buy her.

But Mrs. McKiernan had obviously informed *her* husband of the scene she had witnessed in the kitchen. And Mr. McKiernan adamantly refused to sell Vina. Mr. Gist told Peter that he had better forget about the girl.

"You don't want your children to belong to McKiernan, I can understand that," said Levi Gist. "He doesn't have much of a reputation for kindness to slaves."

"No, sir, he don't," said Peter grimly.

"Whereas," Levi Gist went on, "I seem to have quite a good reputation along those lines. Your children would be well fed, well clothed, not worked too hard. And as you know, Peter, the plantation is prospering. I can just about guarantee you that your family would never be separated. Your wife and children would never be sold. Not as long as I live. And—" he smiled a little— "I plan to keep on living for a good long time."

Peter smiled too, although he didn't much feel like smiling.

"So," Levi Gist summed up the matter simply, "why don't you do like I've always suggested. Marry a girl on *this* plantation. We've got a few that are every bit as fine-looking as Vina."

Peter nodded. And he walked away.

Since it was obvious that Levi Gist would never agree to his marrying Vina, Peter determined to do as his brother had done. He would get married first, and make the announcement later, when it was too late for his master to do anything about it—except, of course, take the cowhide whip from the wall.

But Peter's love for Vina was now so great that he would willingly endure three hundred and seventeen lashes, if that was what Gist's wedding present to him might be.

The question in Peter's mind was no longer whether he should marry Vina, but when.

Finally, that question was answered.

In May 1825, Mr. and Mrs. Gist announced their intention of visiting Lexington. They had a prized new possession that Levi wished to show off to his relatives in Kentucky: their firstborn child, Mary, age five months.

Levi Gist asked Peter whether he would like to accompany them as carriage driver.

But Peter frowned, stammered, and finally said that he did not wish to go. Unless, of course, Master Levi insisted.

Gist was astonished. "I thought there was nothing you would like so well as to go to Lexington and see all your old friends there."

"Well," said Peter, "I expect everybody there has forgot me. It's been so long now."

"All right," said Levi Gist, rather testily. "Then old man Frank can go. He'll not want to be asked twice!"

On a fine May morning, Frank drove the carriage up to the front door. Peter helped strap the trunks on behind, and he stowed away a dozen baskets and bundles on the carriage seat and on the floor. He stood aside watching as Master Levi handed in his wife. The nurse followed with her small charge.

Uncle Frank, dressed in a new suit, proudly climbed up on the box. With a grand flourish of the whip he gave the signal to the spirited horses, and away they went. Levi Gist shook hands with all the servants waiting in the driveway to bid the family good-by. And he embraced his brother-in-law, who was to be in charge of the plantation while the Gists were away. Then he mounted his horse and cantered off after the carriage.

Watching them go, Peter was overcome by the certainty that he had been a fool. The most pleasurable weeks in his life had been spent on the road from Lexington to Bainbridge with John Gist. Now he had not only turned down the chance for a repeat trip, but he would miss seeing the many friends he had in Lexington. And for what? To achieve the very thing he had vowed never to get involved with: marriage.

Yet when he saw Vina that evening, all doubts disappeared like fog in the warmth of sunshine. She was so excited with the idea of marrying at once, that she danced about on the dirt floor of Aunt Lucy's cabin. She had been living there for a month, ever since Martha sickened and could no longer work in the cotton fields. Martha had therefore been taken back as a house servant, and Vina had been sent to replace her in the fields.

"I'm glad I'm out here now," she told Peter. "I wouldn't want to be married and always under the nose of Miss Letitia. Out here we can be more private, as though we really belong to ourselves."

As Peter had fully expected, Mr. McKiernan approved of the marriage. Indeed, McKiernan did more than approve. He promised to supply the food for a wedding supper party in the kitchen.

The wedding was held on a Sunday evening, June 25, 1825. Peter was twenty-five, and Vina fifteen. The bride wore white—and black. All the clothes she had brought with her from Courtland had worn out or had been stolen by other slaves. She had only one dress, a white linsey frock which her mistress had given her the preceding fall. It was ripped, and minus the front breadth. But Peter had given her a black surtout coat of his own, with which she patched the dress. She wore it every day, and since she had no other, she wore it also for her wedding. But Aunt Lucy had fashioned a veil from Mrs. McKiernan's discarded petticoat. It was fastened at the top by a circlet of magnolia blossoms. And when Vina walked slowly from the door of Aunt Lucy's cabin, Peter caught his breath at the sight of her— little Vina, his beautiful bride.

Old Cato Hodge, a Baptist preacher, performed the ceremony. Cato was a slave. But the way he stood tall and dignified, rolling out the words of the marriage ceremony, made Peter feel that this black man belonged to no one but God.

Levin, Peter's best man, stood beside him. And when Preacher Hodge intoned the words, "I now pronounce you, Peter, and you, Lavinia, to be man and wife," Levin handed

Peter a ring he had bought in Bainbridge. "Put this on her finger," Levin whispered. "It's my wedding present to both of you."

The surprise of this present, and the realization that now he was married to the lovely young girl at his side, fused into emotion too strong to contain. He felt for his bride's hand to slip the ring on her finger, but he could barely see what he was doing, for his eyes had filled with tears.

The wedding feast was held in the McKiernan kitchen, with all of McKiernan's house servants, a few of Peter's special friends, and his brother Levin as guests. A long table had been set up, with an entire hog as centerpiece. There were platters of fried sweet potatoes, peas, rice, hot biscuits, garden sass, and even a small quantity of whiskey and rum—all supplied by the McKiernans, who later appeared at the wedding supper to tender the newlyweds their best wishes.

"I never knowed they had this much niceness in them," Vina whispered when her master and mistress had departed.

"Maybe everyone's got some niceness somewhere," Peter told her. "Only in some it's buried down real deep." He felt, however, that he knew well the reason for McKiernan's kindness. He would try now to buy Peter from Levi Gist, and it would be easier if he had the slave on his side, asking for such a sale so that he could spend every night with his wife. But Peter had no intention of asking that he be sold to McKiernan.

After the wedding supper the slaves, sated by food and warmed by drink, moved the party to the field behind the slave cabins. There they were joined by the field slaves from the McKiernan plantation, and from the Gist plantation a mile away. Moonlight cast a faded brightness, and crickets provided soft background sounds as the wedding guests celebrated by singing.

Some of the songs, like *The Rose of Alabama*, were love songs. Peter sat with his arms around his wife and sang the words lustily:

> *"The river rolls, the crickets sing.*
> *The lightning bug he flashed his wing,*
> *And like a rope my arms I fling*
> *Round Rose of Alabama.*
>
> *"I hug so long I cannot tell,*
> *For Rosey seems to like it well,*
> *My banjo in the river fell,*
> *Oh, Rose of Alabama."*

But despite the joyousness of the occasion, most of the songs were sad; for it was sadness, not joy, that had given birth to the song in the first place. One of these mournful refrains came too close, and left Vina weeping quietly.

> *Farewell, old plantation,*
> *Farewell, the old quarter,*
> *An' Daddy, an' Mama,*
> *My poor heart is breaking,*
> *No more shall I see you,*
> *Oh, no more forever,*
> *O-ho! O-ho!*

"I wish that my mama could have been here today," Vina said softly through her tears. "And my brothers."

"Don't you worry yourself," Peter assured her. "You will see your mama again. And your brothers too. Who knows," he added after a moment, "maybe one day I will even see my mother again, and my daddy and my sister Mahala, and my grandmama, though I expect by now that old lady is dead."

"You just saying that," said Vina, "to make me feel good on our wedding night. You don't really mean it."

"Listen here," said Peter sternly, "I don't say what I don't mean. You hear that, missus?"

She smiled at him as though she was beginning to believe.

As Peter took her into his arms he wished suddenly that he had a last name to give her, as a white man gave his name to his bride. But he was still Peter Gist, and she was Lavinia McKiernan. Though Vina now belonged to him, she belonged even more to Bernard McKiernan. It was not a pleasant thought on a man's wedding night.

A few weeks later the Gists returned home.

Peter was not among the slaves who gathered in the driveway to meet them. He was uncertain about what he should say about his marriage. Should he be the first to inform his master of his disobedience? If he did so, he would risk Levi Gist's explosive wrath. If he waited and let Gist learn of the marriage from someone else, perhaps Master Levi would calm down some before he accosted Peter with the matter, and Peter might thus escape a terrible lashing.

As it turned out, Peter did not have to make the decision. As he came in to serve dinner that evening, Levi Gist looked up and said pleasantly, "Well, Peter, so you've stolen a march on us since we've been gone—been getting married, hey?"

"Yes, sir, I—been getting married."

Gist nodded. "Mr. McKiernan wrote me about it when we were in Lexington. He wants to buy you. Would you like to be one of McKiernan's boys?"

"Oh, no, sir," said Peter fervently, setting down the hot platter he carried.

Levi Gist smiled a little. Then he said, "I'm not going to whip you, Peter, as I did your brother. I felt bad about that. I still do. You're free, of course, to see your wife Sunday and any night when your work is done. After all, the Mc-

Kiernans are only a mile away. You can be back here by six in the morning, easy."

"Yes, sir!" said Peter, surprised and delighted at the unexpected kindness, when Levi Gist might well have flown into a fury. After all, Peter had, for the first time, deliberately disobeyed him—even tricked him—by marrying when Gist was away. At least, he had feared his master would see things in that light.

And here was Master Levi saying he could see Vina every night!

Then Levi Gist said, "But there's something you don't know, Peter. And maybe you would not have acted in such haste *had* you known it."

Peter waited. His heart started thudding. Now the punishment would come, something worse than three hundred and seventeen lashes of the cowhide whip. Was he or Vina to be sold? Were they to be separated forever after two weeks of marriage?

"At Christmas-time," said Levi Gist, "Mr. McKiernan plans to sell his plantation. He will buy a new one, but at the moment he is not sure where that will be. If you're lucky, Peter, your wife will be within Sunday–walking distance. But more likely, she'll end up in another county. Or even in another Southern state."

Peter nodded. Then, walking swiftly, he left the room.

Christmas-time. It was now July. He counted slowly on his fingers. He and Vina had six months in which they could be certain of being together. Anything more depended on the business dealings of white men.

# 11

It was a chilly Saturday night in late November. Peter, out of breath from the mile he had run between plantations, opened the door of Aunt Lucy's cabin, and Vina fairly flew into his arms. "We're moving to Bainbridge," she cried with joy. "Only to Bainbridge! Not to Georgia!"

For a time McKiernan had been considering buying a plantation in Georgia; this news, of course, had cast his slaves into a morass of gloom. But now, very suddenly, the master had bought a large plantation just outside Bainbridge. The land contained a large brick house for the owners, and little else. The slave cabins consisted of half a dozen wooden shacks, and McKiernan had thirty-eight slaves. Much of the land was new and had never before been used for farming; the slaves would have to work as they never had before, in order to clear it for planting corn and cotton by springtime.

But whatever the conditions were at Bainbridge, one thing was certain: every one of McKiernan's slaves was deeply thankful that they were not moving to Georgia.

Every Saturday night for the next two months, Peter walked the seven miles to Bainbridge. All Sunday he worked, building a new cabin for Vina. He cut the timber himself, hauled it across the creek, and when the wood was ready, hired men to help him raise it.

He often worked straight through Sunday night when there was enough moonlight to see by. Then Monday at dawn, he would start for home to work the full day through for his master. But Peter was determined to have Vina's cabin finished by the end of December, when the McKiernans would move to the new plantation. He did not want his wife to be crowded in with other slaves in the old shacks.

And when time for the move came, Peter had built a home that was admired even by McKiernan, who straightaway made still another offer to buy this industrious slave. Vina's Cabin, as everyone called it, had a roof of boards, and a chimney of sticks and clay. The floor was made of planks of wood, not the hard-packed dirt that was customary. The only bare ground in the cabin was the hearth.

When Vina first saw the cabin, she turned to Peter with a smile that made all the long hours of work worthwhile. She said softly, "I only wish my mama could see how I'm living now."

The house, however, had nothing in it. Peter cut a walnut tree, hauled it to the mill, and made a fine bedstead. The bedding was a soft pile of straw. Then he went to his Freedom Box hidden beneath the toolshed flooring and, for the first time, he took some money out of it instead of putting money in. He bought his wife an iron pot, two spoons, a knife, two chairs, and a trunk—with a lock—for the items of clothing he had given her since their marriage.

One Saturday night in Bainbridge, he bought a flour barrel, thinking it would serve as a table. But as he was carrying it over the fields he was stopped by Bill Simms, the McKiernans' white overseer.

"I'll have that barrel, boy," said Simms, and he started to take it from Peter, who protested.

Simms spewed out a stream of curses and shoved Peter

aside, "I'll let you know, you damn nigger, you're not to forbid me to take a barrel when I want it."

"But it's mine," Peter insisted. "I bought it, and I'm going to carry it to my wife."

Simms knew that he had no right to whip one of Levi Gist's slaves, and Peter knew that he knew this. But Simms had easy access to revenge. And as Peter walked away with the barrel, the overseer shouted after him, "You'll live to be sorry for this, you damn nigger. You wait and see."

For many weeks Peter worried that Bill Simms, well known for his cruelty, would take out his vengeance on Vina. But when nothing further happened, he assured himself that Simms had forgotten about the barrel, and he tried to put the worry from his mind.

Then, on the twelfth of September, 1826, an event occurred that Peter would have thought was the last thing he wanted. He discovered, however, that it was what he wanted most. Vina gave birth to a little boy. They named him Peter.

Looking down at the infant as he flailed his tiny arms and legs or uttered his lusty cries, Peter was flooded with wonder and joy. He had fathered this new human being. This baby, God willing, would thrive and grow, would become his own eternity. It seemed a more likely way of living on than in the faraway heaven promised by preachers.

When he reflected on the fact that he had so often claimed to himself he never wanted children, Peter would take his new son into his arms and hold him tenderly. More than once he whispered, "Forgive me, little boy."

Vina also regarded this firstborn baby as a kind of private miracle. McKiernan granted every new mother four weeks of freedom from work. This, the slaves knew, was no great act of kindness on their master's part. It was merely that he wanted their babies to live rather than die, for it was the cheapest way to increase one's stock of slaves.

During those four weeks Vina made the little boy tiny clothes. A fine stack of them lay piled in the truck, locked so they would not be stolen by other slaves. She washed the baby carefully twice a day, nursed him whenever he cried, and cradled him in her arms, singing him soft lullabies as he slept.

When the month of this tender closeness was up, the abrupt separation seemed even more cruel. She was permitted to return four times a day from the cotton fields to nurse the baby. But Bill Simms kept a careful watch on the time she was gone. She was given only a few scant minutes with little Peter, time enough only to feed him. Though she longed then to lull him to sleep in her arms, she had to lay him down on the straw mattress and run from the cabin with the sound of her baby's indignant screams following her as she fled.

Often she thought of the days at Courtland when she had served as nurse to a white child. How she would have been whipped had she ever let the white baby scream because of her neglect! But now that her own child needed her constant care, she could not be spared. The cotton must be picked.

When she came home at night, Vina would build a bright fire on the clay hearth and cook her supper. Then she brought water from the spring, undressed the infant, and washed him carefully. Little Peter loved the bathing; he kicked and crowed and laughed. Then Vina would dress him in clean clothes, nurse him, and finally tie him into a chair while she set about her housework. She washed his clothes, hung them up to dry, neatened the cabin, and did mending or washing for her husband. The baby would watch her till his eyelids drooped and he sank quietly to sleep.

When her chores were finally finished, she untied the child and lay on the bed, with little Peter beside her, to sleep. She often reflected that she had never been this happy, and never expected to be. But the height of her happiness came on Saturday nights and Sundays, when her little family was complete.

Sometimes she and Peter dressed in their best clothes and, taking the baby, walked to meeting. But more often they were busy, doing some needed work in the cabin or working in the patch.

McKiernan, as was the practice of other slave-owners, had divided one large field into as many little patches as there were field hands on the plantation. Each slave could work here nights and on Sundays to cultivate his crop. Some raised cotton, others corn, and many gave over their patch entirely to watermelons. The corn and cotton they were obliged to sell to their master—at his price. But the watermelons they could carry to town. This proved the most profitable crop, but it was also risky. Saturday afternoon was the only day on which they could go to market. Yet their freedom to do so depended on the whims of the overseer, and also on whether or not they could borrow a wagon from the master. As a result they often lost large portions of their watermelon crops.

Some slaves also raised chickens, and for these there was always a ready market in the neighborhood.

Since the Gists were understanding about letting Peter leave on Saturday when Vina's watermelons were ready for market, she had planted her whole patch with melons. And between them and Vina's chickens, she and Peter managed to make enough to buy sufficient clothing and extra food.

Vina was the only one of McKiernan's field hands who had enough to eat and enough to wear.

Peter never told his wife about the money he had hidden beneath the floorboards of the toolshed. Nor did he ever confess to her his hope—his ambition—of buying his own freedom. He knew that such a thought would only bewilder and terrify her. Even if he one day succeeded in achieving his impossible plan, it would mean the end of their marriage. To ensure his freedom, as well as his safety, Peter would have to move North. Vina did not know this. But she would soon find out, once Peter told her about his lifetime dream. Time enough to tell her when he had found a white man he could trust to help him. For without the secret help of a white man, nothing could ever be done.

Along with the money, Peter buried the thought of the misery and conflicts that would arise if he were one day able to buy his own freedom. To leave his wife and child. . . . It would be like leaving his life. And yet—to be a free man, owned by no one except himself!

But why dwell on the conflicts? No doubt they would never arise. He now had $78 in his storage box. How old would he be by the time he had earned a thousand dollars, or whatever price his master might set on him? Vina might be dead by that time, and his son Peter a grown man.

One Saturday night when the baby was a year old, Peter came as usual to see his wife and son. But when he embraced Vina, she winced sharply and drew away.

"What is it, girl?" he asked anxiously.

Slowly she undid her frock and stood by the hearth. In the flickering light of the fire, he saw that her back and neck were striped with long, open wounds.

For a long moment Peter simply stood, staring at her,

anger pounding through him with such force that he could not speak. Finally he said, "Who did this to you?"

"The overseer, Simms."

"Why?"

She fastened her dress carefully, so as not to further inflame the searing cuts. "I—I didn't want to tell you . . . for fear what you might do. But for a long time now, that Bill Simms been pestering me to—"

"To what?" said Peter grimly.

"To submit to him."

*You'll live to be sorry for this, you damn nigger. You wait and see.* The overseer's words echoed through Peter's head—words flung out as a threat when Peter had refused to give the white man his barrel. And now the words had turned to whiplashes on Vina's smooth and beautiful back.

"He—he been pestering me a heap," Vina went on. "But I always told him I wouldn't never do no such thing. I told him I'd got a husband of my own, and I wasn't going to have nothing to do with nobody else. He tried to starve me to it. Many a time when he weighed out the food allowance, he never give me half my share. But I didn't mind that. You always bring us food."

She sat down carefully on the chair. "At last he told me if I didn't obey him, he'd whip me nigh to death. I told him he might kill me, but I wouldn't never do it. So when I was in the field today he took and whipped me. He tied my hands with his handkerchief, and pulled my coat off, and then he beat me till I couldn't hardly stand. He struck me over the head mostly, and tried to knock me down with the butt end of his bullwhip. My head is cut in a heap of places."

Still, Peter said nothing. The bile of bitterness rose in his throat.

Vina went on, "When Simms done beating me, he cussed me powerful and said if I ever told the master, or any person so it would get to him, he'd give me a heap more. And if that didn't do, he'd shoot me."

Peter turned. He started out the door.

"Where you going?" Vina rose stiffly and came after him.

"To get old McKiernan down here. Show him what his overseer done to you."

"You can't do that! You know what Master says. If any person come to him with complaints about the overseers, he'd give them worse himself."

Peter did know this, and her words stopped him.

To get McKiernan would mean another whipping, a worse one that might kill his wife.

There was nowhere to turn. No one to go to. Even Master Levi would not interfere in what was regarded as his brother-in-law's business: how McKiernan treated his slaves.

So Peter warmed some water on the hearth, and gently he washed Vina's wounds and bound clean cloth around the deep cuts on her back. The next day, Sunday, he insisted that she remain in bed. He tended her, worked the melon patch, cared for little Peter, and did all the chores as best he could. Vina slept most of the time, and when Peter left her before dawn on Monday, she insisted that she felt "right pert."

But though she continued her work in the fields for two more weeks, she had, she told Peter, "a heap of misery in my head all the time."

And on the third Sunday after the beating, Peter entered the cabin to find Vina on the bed babbling senselessly. He felt her forehead. She had a raging fever.

Terrified, he raced across the fields to the Great House. McKiernan was in his office working on some papers when Peter burst in. This time there was no thought in Peter's mind of who was master and who was slave. He was a man whose wife was dying, and he demanded help. "The doctor! You got to send for the doctor! My Vina, she's out of her head with fever. Please. You got to get help."

McKiernan sent a boy for Dr. Beaumont. Then he hurried after Peter to Vina's cabin.

By the time the doctor arrived, Vina's condition had worsened. Her body seemed aflame with fever, she babbled incoherently, and often she would scream.

Dr. Beaumont examined Vina carefully and gently. Peter realized that this white man did not seem to feel he was merely looking at a slave whose life did not count for much. He paid special attention to the scars and open wounds on Vina's head. And when he had finished, he straightened up and said to McKiernan, "Who whipped this girl?"

It was Peter who answered. He told the full story about Simms, starting from the incident of the barrel. When Peter had finished, McKiernan said, "Why the devil didn't Vina or you tell me about this beating before?"

"I wanted to do that," said Peter. "But Vina—she begged me not to. She told me your rule, that you don't care how hard an overseer beats your servants; if they come to you, they'll get worse from you."

McKiernan glanced at Dr. Beaumont. Then he strode from the cabin.

Meanwhile, the doctor instructed Peter in how to care for his wife. "You must bathe her often with cool water to bring the fever down. But you must bathe her feet in ashes and warm water. If she will drink it, give her warm catnip tea several times a day with a teaspoonful of this medicine in each cup."

He handed a bottle to Peter, who smelled it. The very odor made his eyes smart.

"What's in here, sir?" he asked the doctor.

"It's a special remedy for fevers," Dr. Beaumont said. His voice could not have been kinder or more concerned had Peter been a white man. "It contains camphor, Virginia snakeroot, ipecac, opium, and diluted alcohol."

Peter nodded, frowning a little.

"If this doesn't help," the doctor said, "I'll come back tomorrow with my leeches to draw off some of the poisoned blood."

Again Peter nodded, afraid to ask the question that pounded through his head. *Would Vina live?*

His little son, who had been watching the proceedings with great interest, now started to whimper. And Peter, thankful for the interruption, gave the boy some fruit to eat.

The doctor waited until McKiernan returned with Bill Simms; waited while Peter—on McKiernan's orders—repeated his story; waited while McKiernan demanded of Bill Simms: "Is all this true?"

Simms looked at Peter, his eyes dark with hatred, and slowly nodded.

McKiernan said to Bill Simms, "Leave my place and never come on it again. I will use the wages I owe you to pay the doctor and medicine bills for this girl, and to pay for every day when she is sick and unable to work."

Then Dr. Beaumont said, "She may never be able to work again. In fact, I would consider it a miracle if Vina lives."

# 12

Although everyone expected Vina to die, she did not. Indeed, on June 24, 1828, a year after the brutal beating, she gave birth to another baby. They called the little boy Levin.

Although no one expected Levi Gist to die, he did.

In the spring of 1831, Levi, Thurmuthis, and their three small children took off for a visit to Lexington. There was some question about whether or not Mrs. Gist should go along, for she was carrying their fourth child. But she insisted that she felt perfectly well and wanted to go. It would be a much-needed change.

Four months later she returned home without her husband. He had been stricken suddenly in his parents' parlor, in Lexington. At first it was thought that he had merely fainted. Thurmuthis had knelt down beside him. He was dead.

She described the scene to Peter when she returned home, and they wept together.

Peter's tears were not only for his own master, or for his mistress who had always shown him the greatest kindness, but for his own future as well. What would happen to them now: the thirty-four men, women, and children owned by Levi Gist?

Miss 'Muthis gave birth to her fourth child, a baby who

would never see its father. Then she sank into a state of despondency from which, it seemed, there was no rousing her. She could make no decisions. She seemed not to care about anything.

Her brother-in-law, John, took over the administration of the estate. He had grown into a portly, rather haughty man, and Peter often wondered whether Master John remembered the trip they had taken long ago from Lexington to Bainbridge, when they were merely two young men on the road together and there was little thought of master and slave. If John remembered, he never made mention of it.

He was not a harsh master, and he ran things well, so that life seemed to change little on the Gist plantation. At least, it changed little for the slaves. They settled into their old routines and forgot to be afraid.

One year later there was another death: one which had not been expected, yet when it came no one was very surprised.

Levin had been ailing for some time. He could no longer work in the cotton fields, so he was brought in as a house servant. Around Christmas-time he fell so ill that his mistress told him to stay in bed. When he asked whether his wife could be with him, Miss 'Muthis herself rode to the plantation of James Hogun and persuaded him to allow Fanny to stay with Levin for a few days.

On December 28, Peter had gone to Bainbridge for a Christmas visit with his wife and three small sons. The newest baby, William, was but two months old. That night when he returned to the Gist plantation, he was met by Fanny, who was sobbing. Over and over she told him of his brother's last words.

"Peter!" he had called out with all his strength. "Peter! Oh, Peter!" And then he died.

"It was you he wanted," Fanny wept. "He didn't see me sitting there. It was you he called for at the end before he died."

With Levin's death, something else seemed to die inside Peter: hope.

While Levin lived, there was someone to remember with. Both men had come to believe that they had been born somewhere near Philadelphia, and that they had been born free. Their memories of the cabin, their parents, and their sister Mahala had faded with the years. But while Levin was alive, they could talk about these things. Now that far-off past seemed buried with his brother.

Stark reality set in, and Peter recalled with clarity a memory he had thought was snuffed out by time: two small boys in the hold of a river boat. . . . The old woman called Mother Grace. . . . *Being you don't know where you're from*, she had told them, *might as well be from a free state.* He remembered how she had taught them to say the syllables over and over: *Phil-a-del-fee-yah. Anyone asks you or your brother where you're from, you tell 'em Phil-a-del-fee-yah. Or the countryside nearabouts there. That way they'll know you're a free nigger and not no slave.*

The lifeline of hope, the invisible strength of pride that had always sustained him were based on a trick thought up by an old lady. Perhaps he had been born in a free state. But far more likely, he was the son of slaves.

In any case, what did it matter? He had lived as a slave since the age of six. And he had learned early that even to hint at the dream of some future freedom could mean swift disaster. If anyone reported to his master that Peter was searching for a way to be free, there would be one certain result. From that moment, he would be looked upon as unsafe property. And he would be sold as quickly as possible.

Being sold was the fate Peter and Vina dreaded most of all.

On November 12, 1833, this fate hovered uncertainly over each of the Gist slaves, for Miss 'Muthis married again. His name was John Hogun, and he was a cousin of the notorious James Hogun who ran the "establishment" where Fanny worked as cook.

John Hogun was a widower, twenty years older than Miss 'Muthis. He was ugly, rough-tempered, uncultured, uneducated. But he was a shrewd businessman, and he owned two large plantations. One was only four miles away, the other in Mississippi.

After the marriage, the names of the thirty-four Gist slaves were placed in five lots, arranged in order to keep families together. The first lot would be drawn by Miss 'Muthis and would go with her. The remaining four lots would be drawn by each of the Gist children when they were grown. In the meantime, these slaves would remain on the Gist plantation.

Peter and Vina and their three small sons went to meeting the Sunday before the lots were drawn. They prayed fervently and loudly that he might be left on the Gist plantation. And the lots did fall that way. Not only did Peter remain on the estate, but he was made foreman of the hands, the most responsible position he had ever held. The overseer gave him orders at night concerning the next day's work. In the morning he roused the other workers, then led them into the field. At night he saw to it that their tools were brought back in order and that the people were all in their cabins before he could go to bed. At picking time, he weighed the cotton in each night and reported to the overseer the number of pounds each of the hands had picked. Though he could not write, his memory proved extraordinary. He was never known to give a wrong report.

When the weeks dragged by in their seasonal routine, Peter and Vina tended to forget about the tenuous foundations on which their lives were based.

Then, on a warm June evening in 1839, those foundations collapsed. The Gist slaves were sent into panic by a decree from John Gist. The guardians of the estate had decided to sell the plantation. Some of the slaves would also be sold, and some would be hired out.

After tortured weeks of wondering—would he be sold? —where would he be sent?—Peter was informed that he would be hired to a Mr. Threat, who had a small plantation four miles from Bainbridge. This gentleman was well named. Peter was hired as headman. He worked longer hours than he ever had before. He had no idea what money Threat paid for his labors, for this weekly sum was paid directly to the Gist estate. And since Mr. Threat had no incentive to—as he put it—"fatten up another man's niggers," the food doled out on this plantation was just enough to keep the slaves from starvation.

Mr. Threat saved money on another score. He hired no overseer, nor had he need of one—for his mother, a strapping lady, would ride over the fields every day with a rope and a cowhide whip, which she seemed to enjoy using. If she found a slave not working as she thought fit, Mrs. Threat would dismount from her horse and beat the man.

Vina had fared no better at McKiernan's.

For many years other slave mothers considered her charmed. She had given birth to three children, and they all lived. "Seems like every baby I had," said Vina, "I grew smarter in how to care for it."

But despite the good care, there were always dangers.

In the winter, most mothers of small children built a fire

in the hearth and locked the cabin door to keep the young-sters in and the cold out. But when little William was a few months old, a child in the next cabin burned to death while its mother was working in the field. It was Vina who prepared the small corpse for burial, and ever after she lived with the terror that her little William would be burned to death while she was out in the fields.

During the steaming, hot summer days, locking a child in the cabin was like closing him in an oven all day. Some mothers preferred this to letting their youngsters wander into who-knew-what danger. But Vina left the cabin door open. "Many's the time," she told Peter, "I come home and find my baby sleeping with the sun a beating on its head, enough to addle its brains."

Young Peter, at six, was old enough to feed Levin and the baby. But when Peter and Levin were babies, there had been no one to feed them. So like the other mothers of small children, Vina tied mush in a rag on the child's thumb. When he sucked his thumb, he got some taste of food through the rag. But when she returned from the fields, she always found her children screaming with hunger.

The three boys, however, had managed to survive all the dangers and deprivations. And Vina began to believe what the other mothers said of her, that she was charmed.

When, in the autumn of 1833, she gave birth to a daughter, she looked at the little girl with delight. Sons were fine, and she was proud of hers. But to have a little girl! She doted on the child, nursed her tenderly, and dreamed of the day when little Mahala would be big enough so they could talk together, for talking with a daughter would surely be different from talking with sons.

When she was one week old, the baby developed the croup. Terrified, Vina ran to the master and begged him to send for Dr. Beaumont.

McKiernan was astonished. Dr. Beaumont! To come all this way for the baby of a slave!

But Vina pleaded. She said that she would work extra time on Sundays to pay the doctor bill.

Dr. Beaumont came. He held tiny Mahala upside down. With one hand he grasped her feet, with the other he tickled her throat with feathers soaked in goose grease. The baby vomited; her chest seemed cleared. Then Dr. Beaumont prescribed a medicine that Vina would have to prepare herself, but he gave her the ingredients: licorice root (to be boiled to the thickness of molasses), 2 tsp. vinegar, 4 tbs. strong skunk cabbage root (boiled to strong syrup), ½ fl. oz. tincture of lobelia.

"Give her a teaspoonful of the mixture whenever needed to keep the phlegm loose," the doctor said. Then he left.

While Vina was preparing the medicine, the baby died.

Two years later, Vina gave birth again. She had prayed for a girl, to help her forget the baby Mahala, but a boy was born. They named him Silas. Just before his first birthday, when he had learned to take his first few steps, he came down with a sudden fever and died.

Another two years passed, and Vina gave birth to another daughter. They called her Catharine. She was a beautiful child with huge black eyes and a dimple in her cheek when she smiled. She looked like her mother, and Peter adored her. "I love her double," he told Vina. "Because she's Catharine. And because she's you when you was a little girl."

Catharine lived. But when she was two, another girl was born. They named her Betty. At five months, the infant died, strangled by croup.

In July of the following year a son was born, Bernard. He became the pet of the household, a merry, handsome little fellow who looked as much like Peter as Catharine looked like Vina. But at the age of three, he was seized with spasms and died.

Vina had mourned the death of each of her babies. But she had always managed to submerge her suffering, and be the mother and wife so needed by the other children, and by Peter.

Yet, after the burial of Bernard, she seemed unable to recover. Each Sunday when Peter came to visit, he found her lying on the bed, sometimes staring at the ceiling, sometimes weeping softly. The older boys took care of the chores and looked after six-year-old Catharine.

Peter decided that something dramatic was needed to rouse his wife from her sorrow. One Sunday he took his cashbox from under the floorboards of the Gist toolshed, wrapped it in a burlap bag and carried it to Vina's cabin.

Then he sent the children out to play, locked the door, and ordered his wife to sit up.

Slowly he spilled the contents of the box into her lap, a huge jumble of coins.

She cried out in astonishment. Then she lifted the coins, letting them fall through her fingers. "Peter! Where did you get all this?"

"Doing side jobs," he told her. "Working nights, and sometimes when I couldn't come here Sundays it was to make us some money. Our own private money."

"What we going to buy with all this money?" Vina asked.

Peter took a deep breath. Then he said softly, "Freedom."

She frowned and looked up. Her voice was tight with fear. "You going to use this money for running away? To end up like—like Lewis?"

Lewis had tried it a month ago—running away. They went after him with dogs, who tore him almost to pieces. When they got him home they whipped him, then rubbed him down with spirits of turpentine and pickle juice. There followed more whipping "to beat the medicine in," as the overseer put it. Then Lewis was taken off to the blacksmith's shop for runaway's irons. A fourteen-pound iron ring was welded around his ankle, and one end of a heavy log-chain was fastened to the ring. The other end of the chain was brought up and passed twice around his waist, where it was secured by a lock. An iron collar was then placed around the runaway's neck, and he was sent to the fields and forced to work, though he could scarcely drag himself along.

Lewis's fate was no worse than that accorded to other runaways. And Peter had long since decided that he would never try this route to freedom. He had heard a few stories about an "underground railroad"; but they sounded to him like fairy tales. White folks who would hide a slave and help him on his way to freedom? It was a dream—the way some black preachers dreamed up a splendid heaven where slaves would live with all the comforts of kings, once they had died.

"No," Peter reassured his wife. "I'm never going to be no runaway. I don't want no pack of dogs running after me. I don't want no chains." He dug his fingers through the coins on her lap. "This money is going to *buy* our freedom!"

Vina looked at him, smiling a little. "And just how much does freedom *cost?*"

"Plenty!" he told her. "Because I am planning to buy my freedom, and your freedom, and the freedom of all our children."

Vina nodded. She started putting coins back in the strongbox. "How much you got here now? Maybe enough to buy you a skinny old mule?"

"A lot more than that!" said Peter.

"A hundred dollars?"

"Almost," he said.

"And how long did it take you to earn this almost a hundred dollars?"

He shrugged.

"Twenty years?" said Vina.

He nodded. "Almost."

"So how old will you be before you got the money saved to buy all those freedoms? Old as Methuselah?"

"Almost," said Peter.

They laughed together.

Then Peter took her into his arms. It was the first time he had heard her laugh since the death of little Bernard.

# 13

Peter soon began to realize that the torrent of coins he had poured into her lap had done more than bring Vina back to him.

His own hope, which had lain dead for so long, was now revived. And the terrible conflict was buried. His freedom need *not* mean eternal separation from his wife and children. He had never known the idea was there, until he spoke the words to Vina. If he bought his own freedom, he would make his way north, and there he would somehow earn enough money to buy his wife and children!

It was an impossible plan, of course. But at least—and at last—he *had* a plan for all of his family.

The key to this plan was, as it had always been, meeting a white man he could trust. He vividly remembered the story of the slave Spencer, in Lexington, who had attempted to buy his freedom from three different white men, had been cheated of all his money each time, and had ended up in a slave gang in the Deep South, where he would spend years of his life in chains.

If he, Peter, was ever to find the man he could trust, he was more likely to do so in town than working on a plantation. In addition, if he lived in town, he might find more ways to earn extra money.

He turned to Miss 'Muthis for help.

She was the only white person who had always shown him genuine kindness. Furthermore, she now was able to exert more influence on his behalf.

In the drawing of lots after Levi Gist's death, Peter had "gone" to Miss 'Muthis's daughter, young Miss Sarah, who was still a child. But by October 1842, the child had become a slender young beauty of sixteen. Her eighteen-year-old stepbrother, John Hogun, Jr., fell deeply in love with her. And since they were not blood relatives, the two young people had married, despite some shocked comments made in the neighborhood about Sarah marrying her brother.

The marriage affected Peter's fate and that of the other slaves in Miss Sarah's "lot." Her young husband would henceforth own all her goods, livestock, and slaves. At least he would when he reached the age of twenty-one.

In the meantime, his father would take charge of the property. And his father, of course, was the husband of Miss 'Muthis.

Peter informed his former mistress that his back had begun to hurt him badly. To work any longer in the cotton fields might turn him into a cripple. Could she, perhaps, suggest to her husband that Peter be hired out to a shopkeeper in Tuscumbia or Bainbridge, the two nearest towns?

Miss 'Muthis promised to try.

It took some time. But finally, just before Christmas, Peter received the welcome news that for the following year he would be working for a bookseller, Mr. Allen Pollock, in Tuscumbia.

He was told nothing about his new master, but his imagination took hold. A bookseller! A man who cared about books must care about human beings. When he tried to imagine himself working in a bookshop, he sometimes laughed aloud with the sheer pleasure of the thought. Sweeping the floor, dusting volumes—to a man used to toiling from dawn until sundown in the cotton fields, the vision was pleasurable indeed. Perhaps Mr. Allen Pollock would even teach him to read!

When the first day of the new year finally came, and Peter entered the small shop on Fifth Street, the scene was much as he had imagined it. The store was musty, dusty, lit by the faded daylight pressing in through the small window and the oblong of bright sunlight from the open door. The walls were lined with shelves that contained a scattering of books, piles of old newspapers and magazines, and an assorted collection of quill pens, inkstands, writing tablets, and such.

The shop was empty when Peter entered. He called out, "Mr. Pollock, sir." A curtain parted at the back, and a scrawny-looking old man emerged. He had sharp features and scraggly gray hair and beard. He reminded Peter of an elderly chicken.

"You my new boy?" Mr. Pollock inquired.

"I'm—Peter."

The old man uttered a chuckle and perched upon a high wooden stool. "Well, boy," he said, "let us discuss our business arrangements."

It soon became clear that Mr. Pollock had worked out a way to avail himself of Peter's services free of charge. He had contracted to pay John Hogun $85 a year for Peter. But, as Pollock pointed out, there was not much to do in the shop, so after Peter had cut the wood, swept the store, blackened Mr. Pollock's boots, and attended to his other chores, he was to go out and find work elsewhere in town. He could fix his own prices. But $85 of what he earned, he must turn over to Mr. Pollock. "Anything else you make, boy," said Pollock with a grand wave of his hand, "you can keep."

Peter well knew it was no easy matter to earn $85 from the dimes and half dimes that people paid for chores, and he asked, "What if I don't make that amount of money, sir?"

Mr. Pollock acted as though he had not heard. He leaned forward and said, "There is, uh, one slight problem, boy."

Peter waited.

"I have no room here to keep a slave. But you're welcome to sleep behind the counter. I have an empty packing case. You can keep your things in that."

Peter said nothing, wondering whether he had not, after all, been better off in the fields. As a foreman he'd had his own small cabin, a bed, a table, a chest for his belongings, and a door that he could close and lock shut. The cabin was not his, of course. But at night when he closed the door and locked it, he could at least feel that the place belonged to him.

But now—! To have no *place*. To lie behind a counter in the nighttime!

"Or," Mr. Pollock said, "if you don't take to that idea, boy, I can make arrangements for you at Major Pope's Hotel. I've spoken to them already. They'll give you a room. You can pay for it by washing dishes and the like."

A room! Not a slave cabin. A room in a hotel!

Peter smiled. "Yes, sir," he said. "I would like that."

It was a tiny, airless attic room. The bed sagged in the center. The chest of drawers wobbled on three legs. The window curtains were ripped. But when Peter locked the door and stretched out on the bed, his hands behind his head, and looked around the room—*his* hotel room—a feeling of pride surged through him. A hotel room. Like a man traveling through town. A free man.

And with the pride came hope.

Tuscumbia was a bigger town than Bainbridge. It had many shops, several hotels, a few schools, churches, even a railroad that ran from the town to the boat landing on the Tennessee River. The railroad cars, drawn by mules, had made Tuscumbia an important port for riverboats. Surely there would be many ways to earn extra money in this thriving town. It had taken him years to save the $73.10 collected in his strongbox. But perhaps if he worked very hard he could find ways to make that much money in one year in Tuscumbia.

He did work hard.

He worked many hours each day for Mr. Allen Pollock, and more hours each night washing high stacks of dirty dishes to pay for his room at Major Pope's Hotel. But somehow, in between, he found time to earn extra money. He swept out the classrooms and laid the fires at the Tuscumbia Ladies' School. He did whitewashing. When extra servants were wanted as waiters at a wedding or party, Peter invariably was there. If someone's cook was sick, he took her place. Several shopkeepers hired him by the month to sweep, black boots, take up ashes, and bring water. At times he even dug graves.

But his most profitable jobs came from the Franklin House, the principal hotel in town. Young gentlemen gave frequent parties at the hotel. They hired the hotel rooms and supplied the refreshments, tables, and chairs. And they found Peter invaluable. He would haul in the furniture, set up the food and drinks, and serve them. As the gentlemen left, swaying and staggering through the door in high good humor, Peter would be there to bid them good night, and often to collect a handsome tip for his services. As darkness faded into dawn he could often be seen carrying a table or chairs through the streets, returning them and all other borrowed items to their owners.

Within seven months, he had made the $85 he owed to Mr. Pollock. Whatever else he earned for the remainder of the year would be his to keep.

One hot September afternoon, Peter was passing by a shop with bolts of bright silk foulards, flannels, vestings, and calicos displayed in the window. A man came from the shop, hurried after him, and asked whether he would be free to work one afternoon a week.

Peter looked at the man. He knew well who he was. One of the Jews.

There were two of them, brothers, named Friedman. One was Joseph, the other Isaac. There had been much talk about the Jews when they first arrived in Tuscumbia some six months before. At first, when they opened their dry-goods shop, no customers went in. The Friedmans were the first Jews ever seen in Tuscumbia. But everyone had heard about Jews, how they thieved and cheated. Peter had even heard rumors that Jews had tails.

He was so startled at having been stopped by this Friedman brother that for a moment he simply stared.

The man then said, "My name is Isaac Friedman. My brother and I own the dry-goods shop. You were highly recommended to us. I understand that you hire yourself out by the day. Would you have time to work for us one afternoon a week?"

"Yes, sir," Peter said. Working for a Jew, he reflected, could be no worse than working for Mr. Threat and his evil mother. And if the Jew brothers did not pay him enough, he could always leave. At least he had that much freedom in this new life of hiring out his time.

"Come into the shop," said Isaac Friedman. "We'll talk more about it."

Although the man had spoken to him politely, Peter felt

some apprehension as he entered the store. Maybe the kindly voice was a trick to lure him inside. After all, why had the Jews selected a store just across from the place where slave auctions were held? The brothers owned no slaves themselves; obviously they could afford none. But perhaps they enjoyed standing in their doorway watching, listening, while men, women, and children were sold to the highest bidder.

The shop was clean, and bright with the sunlight that filled the large front window. Peter glanced about, looking for the cowhide whips and mantraps that were usually prominently displayed in stores that sold dry goods and general merchandise. He expected to see new torture devices in the Jew shop. But he saw none. Perhaps they were hidden behind the counter.

Another man came from a side room, and Isaac Friedman introduced his brother, Joseph.

The two men looked much alike. Both had straight, dark hair and deep-set dark eyes. But Joseph was taller than Isaac, and more handsome.

"We're planning to expand our trade somewhat," Isaac Friedman said to Peter. "We'll be carrying some foodstuffs as well as fabrics. Have you had experience in selling?"

"No, sir," said Peter. "But I can learn."

The brothers glanced at each other and nodded slightly.

What were they nodding about? What scheme did they have in mind? He felt wary, yet somehow less nervous. The two men did not *look* evil. But, on the other hand, neither did Mrs. Threat or many other cruel white people he had met.

Their speech was strange. Was this how Northerners sounded? Or foreigners? He had heard the Jew brothers called "dirty foreigners." But he did not know what a foreigner was.

"What day would you be free to come?" Joseph Friedman asked.

"I'm free on Saturdays," said Peter.

"Well," said Isaac Friedman, "we don't open our shop on Saturdays."

"You don't?" Peter exclaimed. "But Saturday's the best shopping day in town. Every shop is open on Saturday."

Isaac Friedman put the heels of both hands on the counter, lifted himself, and sat on it. "In your religion," he said to Peter, "you rest on the seventh day, correct?"

"Supposed to," said Peter, "according to the Bible. But seems like that Bible wasn't talking about slaves when they put down the Sabbath as a day of rest. Leastwise, we don't work on Sundays for our master. Just for ourselves."

Isaac laughed a little. "I know what you mean," he said. Then he continued, "In our religion—the Jewish religion— the Sabbath is on a Saturday."

Peter nodded, but he was puzzled. People said that Jews were greedy for money. Why, then, did they close their shop on the best day of all for making money?

"Are you free any other day?" asked Joseph Friedman.

"How about if I come to you Thursday afternoon?"

"Fine," said both brothers together.

"What rates do you charge?" Joseph asked.

"Two dimes for an afternoon."

"Well," said Isaac Friedman, "if you're as good a worker as I've heard you are, maybe we can do better than that."

Peter looked at Mr. Friedman, astonished.

When he left the shop he felt more confused than ever. If white people, and black, talked so bad about the Jews, there must be a reason—a good reason. But these two brothers had somehow made him feel that he was a man, not a slave. And these two brothers were the first white men who had ever made him feel that way. Even Miss 'Muthis always spoke to him as a kind white mistress speaks to her favorite slave.

On Thursday morning, Peter took the precaution of telling Mr. Pollock where he planned to work that afternoon. Ordinarily, he never let Pollock know where he was going or what he was doing once his chores were finished. But this time he felt he had better take safety measures.

Pollock seemed perplexed. "How come you plan to work for the *Jews?*"

"Why not?" said Peter. He asked the question because he truly wanted to know the answer. Would Mr. Pollock warn him about having his throat slit in the back room in some sort of strange religious ritual? Maybe if he worked there till late at night, the Jew brothers would bury him alive. He waited. Since Mr. Pollock said nothing, he repeated his question: "Why shouldn't I work for them, sir?"

Finally Mr. Pollock shrugged. "No reason, I guess. Matter of fact, that Joseph Friedman comes in here sometimes to buy books. I never saw any harm in him myself. Seems like a decent, hard-working fellow."

"They talk kind of strange," Peter said. "The way they say their words, I mean. They from the North, sir?"

Pollock laughed. "They do talk strange. But not because they come from the North. They're from Germany. Across the ocean. They came to America six or seven years ago."

"And all these six, seven years they did nothing bad?" Peter asked.

Once again Mr. Pollock shrugged. "Nothing I ever heard about."

"Then why is it," Peter persisted, "that people talk so bad about them?"

"Because people are people," said Mr. Pollock. "They like to talk bad—especially about the niggers and the Jews."

The niggers and the Jews!

As Peter walked down the cobbled street, where sewage ran stinking in the gutters, and pigs, dogs, and horses left their droppings, he had a sudden, soaring thought.

Maybe he had found his white man. The man he had been searching for all his life. The man he could trust. Maybe he had even found two men.

If other white men linked them together—"niggers and Jews"—then maybe Jews were different from other white men! Yet, being white, they could own slaves! If one of the Friedman brothers bought him, and then allowed Peter to buy himself. . . .

*Friedman!* Their very name was a good omen!

When Peter entered the shop, Isaac Friedman was sweeping.

"Hello, Peter," he said in a cheerful tone. He put down the broom. "Come. I'll show you around. Then we'll get to work."

He took Peter into the office behind the shop. It was a small room with a rolltop desk, a few simple wooden chairs, and a glass-enclosed bookshelf. Next to it were the living quarters of the two brothers; two small bedrooms, a dining room, and, out back, a kitchen and an outhouse.

Peter's job for the Friedmans would be the same as it was for other shopkeepers, with two exceptions: he was not expected to clean out the latrine, and he was allowed to wait on customers. Isaac Friedman showed him how to measure yardage and how to figure prices. At first he was asked to check all prices with one of the brothers, but by the end of the afternoon they told him that he had a fine head for figures and he need not check with them further on prices, unless he felt the need to do so.

When he left the Friedmans that night he was elated. Not only had he learned a lot, but they paid him double what he had asked. And never once during all those hours had either brother called him "boy."

The following Sunday he told Vina that he had "found his white man."

But she was skeptical. Not because the Friedmans were Jews—she had never even heard of Jews. But because the Friedmans were white. She had heard too many tales through the years of white men who could be "trusted."

"Trusted, yes!" she burst out. "Trusted to get you put in chains!"

Peter nodded. "Look," he said slowly. "I'm in no big hurry. No use me telling the Friedman brothers my freedom plan till I got me at least $500 saved up. Don't need them to hold my money for me, the way old Spencer gave his savings away to white men. I'll save it myself in my own strongbox. And in the meantime I'll be watching those two men, testing them out to see if they are the men to trust."

# 14

At Christmas-time in the year 1846, Peter went to call on his young master. John Hogun, Jr., had now come of age and had taken over control of his wife's property, Peter included.

"I know Mr. Pollock's planning to hire me again, sir," said Peter. "But there's Mr. Joseph Friedman, sir. If you hire me to *him* for the year, he told me he'll pay you more than what Mr. Pollock pays you."

"The *Jew?*" said young John Hogun, astonished. "The Jew will pay more than Mr. Pollock?"

Peter nodded. "So he has told me, sir."

"And you don't object to working for the Jews?"

"No, sir," said Peter. "Seems like they won't work me so hard as Mr. Pollock does. And with my bad back, sir, and my bad cough, I'm not in fit condition to be worked too hard." And he promptly went into a fit of coughing.

Peter had, in fact, neither a bad back nor bad cough. But this claim would fit into his plan.

At the start of the new year, he went to work for the Friedman brothers. The arrangement was much the same as had been made with Mr. Pollock, but with one important difference: Peter did not have to pay back to the Friedman brothers the sum of money that they paid to Hogun to hire him. Yet, when his duties in the shop were finished, Peter was free to get whatever work he could, and to keep whatever money he made.

By the end of the year, he had $210 in his strongbox. The Friedmans hired him for another year, and he began it with his hopes higher than ever before.

In all the days he had known them, the two brothers had said nothing, done nothing to make him waver in his judgment that he had finally found the white men he could trust. Indeed, the more he came to know them, the closer were the bonds he felt, especially when he learned that the Jews themselves had once been slaves.

He told Vina and his children about it with high excitement.

"They have a Jewish holiday, Passover. They told me not to come to work. And when I asked what this holiday is all about, they told me it's to celebrate old man Moses leading his people out of slavery."

"*White* people was *slaves!*" ten-year-old Catharine exclaimed.

"The *Jews* was," said Peter. "Long ago, before Christ was born. They was slaves to the Egyptians. They got whipped just like we do. They worked just as hard—harder, maybe. They had to haul big stones around. Mr. Isaac showed me pictures in a book. Stone tombs higher than a house. Made by these slave Jews."

"What we need," said Vina, "is a black old man Moses to lead *us* out of slavery." But after learning that the white Jews had once been slaves, she said no more about not trusting the Friedman brothers. She seemed to accept Peter's conviction that these were the men who would help him.

Now that he was certain he had found the way, Peter worked harder than ever. Sometimes he had no more than three or four hours of sleep a night. His money box grew so full and heavy that he took to carrying coins about with him in a leather purse that Vina had made for him. It was twelve inches long, three inches wide at the bottom, and half that width at the top. He kept the bag in his trousers pocket, beneath the loose blue roundabout he always wore. Sometimes, especially when working in hotels, he would see a piece of gold in the hands of a man he had served. He always asked whether said gentleman would give him the ten- or twenty-dollar gold piece in exchange for silver coin. The gentleman would generally oblige, always with the obvious assumption that the coins Peter poured from his leather purse were the sum of his lifetime savings.

Then, in the winter of 1848, Peter overheard something that made him realize he would have to speak to the Friedmans about his plan right away. Joseph Friedman was planning to move to Texas or California! What if Isaac went too? What if Peter finally saved up his $500 in freedom money—and the only two white men he trusted had left town!

That very evening he knocked at the door of the office and was asked to enter. Joseph Friedman sat by the fireplace reading a magazine to which he subscribed. It was, he had told Peter, edited by a Rabbi—a Jewish preacher—and sent to thousands of Jewish subscribers throughout the country. But he kept the issues locked in his desk. "Our white friends and neighbors," he had once told Peter, "might not approve of some of the sentiments in this publication."

Now, as Peter entered, Joseph Friedman looked up from his magazine, the *Occident*.

For a moment Peter could not speak. His head throbbed painfully, and his knees trembled. This plan, which he had held secret for so long, was about to be exposed for the first time, to a man who could destroy it. A white man, who could destroy *him*.

"What is it, Peter?" asked Joseph Friedman. "Sit down. You have something on your mind?"

"But—it's a great secret, sir."

Mr. Friedman nodded. "Sit down," he said again.

Peter sat. But still he could say nothing.

"Well, Peter—?"

"I've been thinking, sir—" the words were blurted out all at once—"I'd like to buy myself. And you've always dealt so fair with me, I didn't know but you might buy me, and then give me a chance to buy myself from you."

Mr. Friedman looked rather startled. Then he laughed and repeated the plan in his own words, sounding baffled but pleased. "I am to buy you from your master. And when you're my slave, you give me the money I paid for you, and I give you your freedom. Is that correct?"

Peter nodded.

"Well," said Mr. Friedman, "it's an interesting plan. But I happen to know that a few men in town have offered your master as much as $800 for you. He wouldn't sell. He said you were worth a lot more."

"I've got $300 saved already, sir. And maybe you can get him down in his price."

"You've heard that about Jews, have you?" said Mr. Friedman wryly. "And how did you manage to save up $300?"

"I been working and saving ever since I was grown," said Peter. "Saving for my freedom. I figure in another two years, working like I am now, I can have $500. If you're willing to help me, sir, I'm certain you can get my price down to $500."

116

Mr. Friedman laughed again and slapped his knee. Then he stood up. "Well, Peter!" he said, "at least we'll try!"

Joseph Friedman rode out to the plantation to see John Hogun, Jr. And he returned with the report that neither Hogun nor his wife, Sarah, had the slightest intention of selling Peter. "Told me," said Friedman, "if he ever did sell the 'boy,' that was no price for him. He'd bring twice that sum." Then Friedman smiled, but there was sadness in it. "And how old does a slave have to be," he asked, "not to be called 'boy' any longer?"

"Old enough to be 'uncle,'" said Peter. "I'm forty-eight, Mr. Joseph. To some I'm 'boy,' to some I'm Uncle Peter." Then he asked, "Did you tell Master John about my bad cough?"

"I did, indeed," said Friedman. "I told him if you belonged to me I would try to cure your cough. I told him if you were not cured, you'd soon be worth nothing to anyone."

"And he paid you no mind?" said Peter.

Friedman shook his head. "For a thousand dollars, he'll sell you. Not for less."

"Maybe," said Peter, "if Master John hears my cough, instead of just hearing *about* it. . . ."

"All right," said Friedman. "Try it yourself. Go there and cough up a storm."

The following Sunday, instead of walking to see Vina, Peter took another road and went to the Hogun plantation.

There he confronted his young master with a great, whooping spasm of coughing that left him faint and gasping.

"Master John Henry," he managed when he had regained his breath, "I come to see you about Mr. Friedman buying me. He said he named you a price of $500."

*117*

"So he did," said Hogun. "But I can get a thousand for you any day."

After another fit of coughing Peter said rather faintly, "I think you're mighty hard to ask such a big price for me when I been in your service so long. Miss Sarah's got all my earnings ever since I belonged to her great uncle, Master Nattie Gist. Now, when I'm almost fifty years old, I think $500 is enough for me."

"Well, Peter," said Hogun, frowning, "people like to get all they can for their property. And it makes no difference to *you,* anyhow, whether I sell you for a big price or a little one."

"Yes, sir, it does," Peter exclaimed. "If a person gives a thousand dollars for me, he's going to work it out of me. But Mr. Friedman just wants me to wait on him about the store."

"I don't want to sell you," said John Hogun crossly. "I'd rather bring you home here to drive the carriage than to sell you for any such price. Go back to town now, and stay there till I come see about you."

Peter nodded, said his good-bys, and then he mumbled, "Seems like I'm fated to die early. Just like my brother, Levin."

He left, coughing loudly all the way down the front walk.

On the way back to town he walked slowly, scuffing his feet in the dusty roadway. His destiny lay clenched in the fist of a young man of twenty-three. He had hoped for so long. He had come so far. And now, suddenly all seemed as hopeless as ever.

On the first of the year, he was hired out once more to the Friedman brothers. And ten days later, on a chill and windy morning, John Hogun, Jr., ambled into the dry-goods shop. Peter, who was behind the counter folding up yards of calico, immediately began coughing.

Hogun asked for Joseph Friedman. Between gasping spasms, Peter indicated that Joseph was out. But Mr. Isaac was in the office.

"Fetch him, then," said John Hogun, Jr.

When Isaac came out, Hogun informed him in an off-hand way that an auction was being held that afternoon of certain goods: the property of his late uncle, old Jimmy Hogun.

Peter caught his breath. Old Jimmy Hogun, dead! Fanny's master. What would happen to her now?

He soon found out. Hogun's ten slaves would be auctioned off with the other goods.

"There'll be two boys up for sale that I want," John Hogun said to Isaac Friedman. "If you'll go in and bid off one of the boys for me, I will let you have Peter in exchange."

Hope burst through Peter's chest. But he kept on folding calico, coughing quietly.

"I'll—think about it," said Isaac carefully. "How high will the boys go?"

"I don't know. They're not worth as much as a tried hand like Uncle Peter. Step in, and see how the sale goes on."

He left the store. And Isaac, exultant, turned to Peter. "You see! We still have a chance!"

But Peter was wary. "You're not used to dealing in slaves, sir."

"Well, that is certainly true," said Isaac. Though auctions were held directly across from the shop, the brothers never attended when slaves were to be sold.

"You'd best not buy the boy," said Peter. "There'll be some game about it. If young master wants to buy him, he'll come around, I reckon."

For an hour the two men barely spoke. It was as if each

*119*

was holding his breath. Would John Hogun, Jr., return?

Shortly before noon Hogun came back.

"I won't buy the boy," said Isaac Friedman firmly. "But I will pay $500 for Peter. Use that money to buy the boy yourself."

"Five hundred is no price for a servant like Peter," young Hogun exploded. Then, after a long moment, he added, "You can have Peter for six hundred. Though he's worth much more."

"No," said Isaac. "I will not pay six hundred."

John Hogun, Jr., slammed out of the store.

The auction was scheduled for two that afternoon. At one o'clock the ten slaves, chained together in a coffle, were brought outside by the auction block so that potential buyers could look them over. Peter went out to see whether Levin's wife Fanny was there.

She was not. He spoke to one of the women, who told him that Fanny had been sold last week to a planter in Mississippi. Then a white man came and ordered the woman to strip so that he could see what it was that he planned to buy. "It's right cold, sir," she protested.

The autioneer overheard this. "Now, Annie," he said in a smooth voice, "You do what the gentleman asks. Ain't you proud to show him you've got hardly a whip mark on your whole body!"

Peter left and went back to the shop.

Fanny. The wife of his dead brother. Sold to some planter in Mississippi.

At two o'clock, when the auction began, Peter stood in the doorway of the shop. Usually he and the Friedmans closed the door when a slave auction was held across the way. But this time the auctioneer's chant might be echoing his own future.

A young boy was the first to be put on the block. Was this one of the boys John Hogun wanted?

"Gentlemen!" The auctioneer's voice commanded silence from the crowd, some of who had come to buy. Others attended every slave auction simply to see the show. "This afternoon," the auctioneer bellowed, "I'm going to sell you as likely a nigger as ever you seen put up. Twelve years old and sound as a dollar! In four years, he'll be bigger'n me and worth a thousand dollars in any market, if he's worth a cent. He can hoe corn or cotton, drive, wait table, run errands, learn any trade. Now, who'll say five hundred. . . ."

"Five hundred," someone called from the back.

"Thank you. Now, Colonel, will you make it five-fifty. . . . Fifty I have. Say six; make it six hundred. Thank you, Judge. Six hundred is bid. But he's worth three hundred more."

As he rattled off figures, sputtered phrases, swept every face with his rapid glance, gesticulating, clapping his hands, the auctioneer drew forth bids that climbed slowly by fives and tens. "Seven hundred and five!" he shouted. "Once . . . twice . . . third . . . and *last* call. Going, *going*—SOLD for $705 to this fine gentleman here."

Suddenly Peter saw John Hogun break from the crowd. He came hurrying across the street.

"Mr. Isaac!" Peter knocked at the office door. "Come out quick, sir!"

Hogun rushed into the shop. "Well!" he exclaimed as Isaac Friedman stood waiting. "You may have Peter for $550."

Isaac glanced at Peter, who shook his head very slightly.

"I will give you $500," said Isaac firmly. "My brother authorized me to pay that sum and no more."

"But—" Hogun protested, "I've been offered $800 for Peter."

"That was before he got sick," said Friedman.

John Hogun glanced out the door. The other young boy was now up on the block.

"I will give you $500!" Isaac Friedman said loudly. "Not one dollar more."

The auctioneer had started the bidding.

"Yes. All right. Five hundred," said Hogun. "Can you have the money for me tomorrow?"

"I can," said Friedman.

Young Hogun ran out of the dry-goods shop and back across the street to the auction block.

Peter and Isaac stood in the doorway watching, as Hogun bid off the boy for $750.

"Well, Peter!" Isaac Friedman exclaimed. "At last, you're on your way!"

# 15

Late that same night, Peter stood before the closed door of Isaac Friedman's office. The leather bag, which he carried with him always, was now bulging. And the strongbox that had been hidden for years under the floorboards of Vina's cabin was empty save for a scattering of coins.

After Hogun's promise to sell him, Peter had gone at once to get the money. But now that he was about to hand it over to a white man, Vina's words flooded through his head.

"How you know you can trust him?" Vina had cried out. "When you ever hear of a white man you could trust? He's going to take your money and buy you with it! Then you belong to the Jew 'stead of Master John Hogun, and you be the same off as before except with a new last name. The name of a Jew!"

"I've known Mr. Friedman a long time," Peter told her. "And I've never known him to do a mean trick. If I can't trust *him*, the Lord help me! I can't never be free without trusting some person, anyhow."

Yet, now that he was about to give his lifetime savings to the white man, it was Vina's doubts which sounded stronger within him than his own reassurances.

He took a deep breath, knocked on the door.

"Come in," Mr. Friedman called.

Peter entered. He took the leather bag from beneath his shirt. He untied it. And slowly he spilled the contents on the desk top. There were pieces of silver, of all sizes, and an occasional gold piece that glittered in the lamplight. Coins that represented thousands of hours of drudgery, and years of secret hoping. . . .

"Three hundred dollars, Mr. Friedman," Peter said softly. They counted the money together; counted it twice.

Then Mr. Friedman took a pen, wrote some words on a sheet of paper which he handed to Peter. "A receipt," he said. "Received from Peter Hogun, the sum of three hundred dollars. Signed Isaac Friedman. January 14th, 1849."

Peter folded the paper and put it into the empty leather purse.

The next day Joseph Friedman returned home from Texas. When he heard the startling news, he embraced Peter. Then he said, "God must be with you. I went to Texas with some money to put as down-payment on a new store. If I *had* done so, we'd not have the $200 we need when Hogun comes with his bill of sale. But—" he laughed a little— "no one there would sell a store to a Jew. That was fortunate, as it turned out."

A few hours later, young Hogun came to the shop. Joseph Friedman gave him the $500. And Hogun gave Friedman a piece of paper.

$500. For the consideration of five hundred dollars, paid to me this day, I have sold to Joseph Friedman, a Negro man named Peter. I bind myself and heirs to defend the title of said Negro, Peter, to the said Joseph Friedman and his heirs against all claims whatever.

Given under my hand and seal this 15th January, 1849.
JOHN H. HOGUN.

When Hogun had gone, Joseph Friedman read the bill of sale slowly to Peter. Then he said, "I'm sure you'd like a copy of this to keep, and to show your wife."

And he made a careful copy of the bill of sale, which he handed to Peter.

The emotion shown by the brothers was so genuine that Peter lost any thought he had held about being tricked. When he showed the bill of sale to Vina, he declared that the Friedmans were the kindest and most honorable white men he had ever met.

He was astonished, therefore, when he went back to Tuscumbia on Monday morning and discovered that the news of the sale had spread around town, and that great sympathy was felt for "poor Uncle Peter." Why, he was asked many times, would Hogun sell such a faithful servant—to a *Jew?* Peter was warned that the Friedmans wanted only to make money out of him. After "jewing" Hogun down in his price, the brothers would sell Uncle Peter for all they could get. Perhaps he'd be taken off to work in the rice swamps. "Jews," he was told by several irate citizens of Tuscumbia, "will sell their own children for money!"

The Friedman brothers informed Peter that he no longer needed to work for them. "From now on," said Joseph, "your time is your own. Go where you like, and earn all you can for yourself."

For the first time Peter truly felt like a free man.

In his own eyes he took on a new dignity. And this was reflected in the eyes of his wife and children. The three boys and Catharine had now been told of their father's plan. And Peter had promised them that his freedom would lead the way to theirs. "But," he warned, "none of you must marry. It will be hard enough to raise the money to buy freedom for five. And—" he looked straight at his oldest son, "you surely won't be wanting to leave a wife and children behind when I send for you to come and join me up North."

Young Peter, now twenty-three, was much taken by a girl named Susanna. But he reluctantly promised his father that he would not marry.

None of the children believed that their father's promises would ever come to pass. Still, he was on his way to becoming a free man. And who would ever have believed that *this* could happen?

One warm Sunday in July the third son, eighteen-year-old William, went fishing on Spring Creek, just below the town of Tuscumbia. By evening he had not returned.

Peter went out to look for the boy. He returned at nightfall, carrying the body of his drowned son.

William was buried on the hillside beside the graves of little Silas, Betty, who died at the age of five months, three-year-old Bernard, and the infant Mahala, who died when she was one week old.

Vina was crushed by the death of William, her favorite son. "To think of his struggling and going down there all alone." She wept, repeating the words over and over. "Seems like it's more than I can bear." She became convinced that William's death was a sign from God, a warning. Worse might befall the family were Peter to persist in his stubborn plan to upset the way things were, and perhaps were meant to be. And how could she bear to let her man go, so soon after losing her son?

Peter assured her it would not be so soon. It had taken him years to save up the $300. It would take many more years to earn the additional $200 he needed.

It did not, in fact, take years. Since he could now keep all the money he earned, the coins accumulated quickly.

On September 1 Peter was able to pay Joseph Friedman $100. He had made the money in eight months.

The following March 29, he gave Friedman $60.

And late in the evening of April 16, 1850, Peter knocked on the door of the Friedmans' small office. His hand trembled as he raised the latch.

"I—I have it," he said to Joseph Friedman, who sat at the desk. "The rest of the money."

He took out his worn leather purse, spilled its contents onto the desk top.

The shop door opened, closed. Footsteps. It was the auctioneer. He walked into Friedman's office.

Quickly Friedman laid a pile of papers over the coins. But the man had seen.

"What, Peter?" he said. "Are you paying up your hire money?"

"Yes, sir. Master Joe make me pay him up close."

"That is so," said Friedman. "Peter must pay me promptly."

"Well, that's the best way," said the auctioneer. "Look, Friedman, I came in to ask whether you're ready yet to sell Peter. There'll be a slave auction on Tuesday. I might get you double what you paid for the boy."

Joseph Friedman shook his head. "I didn't buy Peter to sell him."

"No?" The auctioneer sounded surprised. "I heard different."

"Things are not always as we hear them," said Mr. Friedman.

The auctioneer shrugged. "Well, if you change your mind. . . ." He said a polite "good evening" and left the shop.

Joseph Friedman went to the front door and locked it.

Then he carried a wooden chair into the office and asked

Peter to have a seat. "I want you to watch as I write." He took up his pen, and he spoke each word aloud as he set it down on paper.

"Received, Tuscumbia, January 14th, 1849, of Peter—" He looked up, frowning. "You *have* no last name?"

"No slave has a last name," said Peter. "Only the name of the man he belongs to. I'm Peter Friedman now."

"When you leave this office, you won't be Peter Friedman. You will be Peter—a free man. Then you can choose your own last name."

Now that the moment had come, Peter did not believe it. He was numb. He felt nothing. Calmly he suggested that Mr. Friedman write down the words "received of my slave Peter."

But Friedman refused. "I'll never put those words on paper. *My slave.*"

"But," Peter protested, "if the paper don't sound like you was my master, it won't sound like you're giving me freedom."

Joseph Friedman agreed. Slowly, carefully, he wrote:

Received, Tuscumbia, January 14th, 1849,
    of my boy Peter, three hundred dollars . . . . $300.00
          *Jos. Friedman*

Received September 1st, 1849, of my boy,
    Peter, $88.00
Eighty-eight dollars and twelve dollars,
    $12.00 . . . . . . . . . . . . . . . . . . . . . . . . . . . . $100.00
Received March 29th, 1850, of Peter, sixty
    dollars, . . . . . . . . . . . . . . . . . . . . . . . . . . . $60.00
          *Jos. Friedman,*      $460.00

Received, April 16th, 1850, forty dollars, . . . . . . . $40.00
                                 $500.00

For, and in consideration of the above five hundred dollars,
I have this 16th day of April, 1850, given Peter a Bill of
Sale, and given him his freedom.

JOSEPH FRIEDMAN

*Tuscumbia, Ala., April 16th, 1850.*

"This," said Peter, pointing to the last sentence, "please,
sir, would you read it again?"

Friedman did so.

"And again."

Friedman read the words once more.

Then Peter repeated the phrase slowly: ". . . and given
him his freedom . . . and given him his freedom . . . his—
freedom." He said the words, but still he could not feel
them. For so many years he had waited for this moment.
For so many years he had worked for it, never fully expect-
ing it to come. He was sitting on a wooden chair, the same
as he had been a few minutes before. Except not the same.
A few minutes ago he had been a slave. And now he was
free. He belonged to no man, except himself. But he felt the
same. Nothing had happened.

He saw tears on Joseph Friedman's cheeks. The white
man was weeping. But he, Peter, felt nothing at all.

"Thank you, sir," he said.

He got up and walked to the door.

"Wait," said Friedman. "Don't you want this? Your certificate of freedom."

Friedman came to him, gave him the paper. Then, wordlessly, he shook Peter's hand.

And Peter walked out into the soft springtime night.

# 16

Later that night, lying on his bed in the small attic room of Major Pope's Hotel, he came to understand what the trouble was. He was afraid to be free.

The piece of paper folded in his leather pouch was a key that opened the world to him. He could go where he wished.

And he knew, of course, where it was that he wanted to go. Philadelphia. The city that lay in the free state called Pennsylvania, somewhere up North. Somewhere . . . but *where*? And how would he get there? And what would he do there?

His family. His mother . . . daddy . . . they were no doubt dead. He had made up a dream for himself as a child. A child needed a dream. But he, like a fool, had clung to this dream until he was fifty. And now did he expect to go all the way to Philadelphia searching for a dream he had made up when he was six years old?

And that other dream. . . . In the North, as a free man, he would somehow make enough money to *buy* Vina from McKiernan . . . to buy his sons, Peter and Levin . . . and his daughter Catharine. The children had never believed him when he promised them this. Vina had never believed him. They had pretended, that was all. And they were right not to believe.

What could he do if he did get to Philadelphia? Get a job washing dishes in a hotel, maybe. Or waiting on tables. Or as a cook . . . or a field hand . . . even a grave-digger. But how much money could he make at such jobs? Perhaps after years of working and saving, he would have enough money to buy his wife. *If* McKiernan would sell her. Even so, would Vina leave her children, their children?

Was it not better to remain here, keeping his freedom a secret? At least he would be with his family. And if Vina were sold, he could follow her. Wherever she was, he could go there. Because he was free.

Yet, if he had even a threadlike chance to save his wife and children from slavery, was he not obliged to try? At least, to try. . . .

For how many years had he dreamed of this time, these first hours as a free man? He had wondered how he would contain his exploding joy. Instead, he felt turmoil, and fear.

At dawn the next morning he went to the Friedman Brothers Dry-Goods Shop. He went there for no reason.

The shop was locked.

He sat outside by the front door and waited. For no reason. He sat staring at the auction block across the street.

Finally he stood up, looked in the front window, and saw Isaac Friedman entering the shop from his bedroom at the back.

Peter knocked on the window. Friedman waved to him and unlocked the front door. "Peter!" he said warmly. "Come in. Have some coffee. My brother and I have been making plans. Do you have time to talk now?"

It seemed that Isaac Friedman had decided to visit Cincinnati, where his brother Levi lived. As he stirred sugar into his coffee he said to Peter, "I know that your plans are to go to Philadelphia, but maybe we could take the river trip together. And, of course, if you'd like to stop off first in Cincinnati for a while. . . ." He let the sentence hang.

But Peter understood all that was left unsaid.

Isaac Friedman knew his fear, and was offering him help, without seeming to do so.

And Peter accepted his help, accepted it as a free man. "When you planning to leave?" he asked.

"Could be any time. When would be good for you?"

"Soon as I make me seventy, eighty dollars," said Peter. "Maybe around the middle of July."

The following morning as Peter was sweeping the floor of Pollock's bookshop, Isaac Friedman entered. He asked for Mr. Pollock.

"He's not here, sir," said Peter politely. "Can I help you?"

"Is there—anyone else in the shop?"

Peter shook his head. "I'm here alone."

Mr. Friedman relaxed. "I've come across some information, Peter." His voice was concerned. "I wanted to check that all was in order. I've been looking into the local law books. A slavery act was passed in Alabama in 1833."

"I'm—not free?" Peter whispered. Was he to be another Spencer? Tricked by the one man he thought he could trust?

"You're free so far as I'm concerned," said Isaac Friedman. "But according to Alabama law, it seems it's not quite so simple."

Peter nodded, afraid to hear more. He picked up the broom and started sweeping. He was thankful only that he had not yet told Vina and his children. "What's the law you found out?" he asked grimly.

"Well," said Friedman, "it seems that any owner who

wishes to free a slave must first publish in the county paper the time and place he plans to make application to the court announcing that he wishes to emancipate one of his slaves."

Peter kept sweeping. He did not know the meaning of the sentence Isaac Friedman had spoken. But he knew the meaning of the man's tone of voice: it meant he, Peter, was still a slave.

"In the application," Friedman went on, "the master must also describe the slave he wishes to emancipate. Then the application must be heard by the county court. And only if the judge agrees that the slave may become a free man—only then, Peter, does the freedom certificate count."

Peter stopped sweeping. He leaned on the broom handle and stared at Isaac Friedman. But he saw only a figure blurred by his own tears. The Jew had not tricked him, he was certain of that. He believed the concern in Isaac Friedman's voice. But the court would trick him. The judge would trick him. He was certain of that too.

And it appeared that Friedman was thinking the same thing. "If I were not a Jew," he said bitterly, "there might not be trouble with your application. But, Peter, I am fearful that if your case comes before a local judge, things won't go well for you. Or for me either, if it comes to that. People resent us enough as it is. And if we, the Friedman brothers, become the first men in town to allow a slave to buy his own freedom—"

Friedman said no more, but Peter understood his silence more clearly than his words.

"Even if, by some miracle, the judge did grant you your freedom," Friedman went on, "it could only be done, according to Alabama law, on the condition that you move out of Alabama and that you never return. Furthermore, you would be a slave until you left the state."

"So freedom," said Peter, "is not a matter between a slave and his master. It is something some other man must decide. Some stranger."

Friedman nodded. "In this state, yes. That is how the law reads. But perhaps up North in Cincinnati, the certificate would have meaning."

"You're saying I should come with you, sir? The way we planned it yesterday?"

"I'm saying I will do all I can to help you," Friedman said simply. "But it is your life, Peter. And your decision. If you leave Alabama, you will never be able to come back to your wife and children again."

It was a sunny blue afternoon, July 20, 1850, when "Master Isaac Friedman and his slave Peter" boarded the boat for Cincinnati. The name of the boat was *The Greek Slave*. Peter hoped the name was not an omen.

His freedom certificate was carefully sewn into his coat pocket. It was a secret to all except Vina, the children, and the Friedman brothers. The three Friedman brothers.

The third brother, Levi, lived in Cincinnati. He had, at Isaac's request, investigated the matter of freeing a slave. And he had written Isaac that Peter's freedom certificate could pave the way toward an official legal document signed by the mayor of Cincinnati. This would mean nothing in Alabama. But it would at least protect Peter from the slave-catchers who roamed through the Northern states hunting for runaways, whom they arrested and brought back South to their masters.

Peter had decided to put his fate and his future in the hands of the Friedmans and the mayor of Cincinnati.

He paid his fare on *The Greek Slave* by working as a waiter in the dining salon. At mealtimes he forgot his mounting fears, worries, loneliness. He was caught up in the pulse and elegance of life on board. Ladies, splendidly attired, jewels sparkling, skirts rustling as they swept by; bearded gentlemen in top hats and frock coats; the soft blue smoke of their after-dinner cigars; the wild, gay strains of a calliope on the upper deck, heralding the boat's arrival at a landing. . . .

But at night Peter lay on a slab of board in the crowded servants' quarters below deck. It was oven-hot there, and stank of sweat. When he closed his eyes, he often felt he was falling backward through his life . . . to the last time he had been on a boat. The same hot darkness and stench. The fears of a fifty-year-old man were heightened by the remembered terrors of a six-year-old boy.

Early on the morning of July 26, the boat neared Cincinnati, a city set in the semicircle of two green hills ribbed by terraced vineyards. Distant church spires seemed painted by sunlight.

Levi Friedman was waiting for them at the Public Landing, a tall, slender, well-dressed gentleman who wore a top hat and carried a cane.

The brothers embraced. Then Isaac said, "Levi, meet Peter."

Levi Friedman put out his hand. Peter hesitated. Then Levi grasped Peter's hand, shook it warmly, and said, "Welcome to Cincinnati."

"Thank you, sir," Peter answered softly.

Levi Friedman had a carriage waiting, and Peter sat inside next to the two brothers. Excitement churned within him. Cincinnati was the largest city he had ever seen. Streets were lined with trees, and with shops of every variety. The signs above some of the shops looked strange. When Peter asked Mr. Isaac about this, both brothers laughed. "That's German," said Levi Friedman. "Cincinnati has a population of 150,000. Of that, almost half are Germans. And more keep coming in all the time. We speak German at home. But," he added, "we won't today, since we have a guest who doesn't know the language."

An hour later, Peter was startled to learn that the "guest" was himself!

The mother of the Friedmans, a stout, friendly woman with a heavy German accent, showed him into a room where he could wash up from his trip. There was warm water in the pitcher, a bar of yellow soap, a clean towel.

"Come to the dining room when you are ready," she said.

When he went downstairs, the family was gathered, talking together in the strange language that must be German. He hesitated in the doorway. Was he expected to sit with them, as he had in the carriage? Or to wait on them?

Levi saw him. "Ah," he said, "Our guest has arrived." And Peter found himself seated at the table with the family. Even more startling, they were all served by a white girl, who spoke with still another accent. Her name was similar to that of his own daughter: Kathleen.

Levi and his mother seemed intensely interested in Peter's stories about his past, and in his plans for the future. He was, for the first time in his life, the center of white people's attention. His sense of inner security expanded, and as he spoke he found that his own feeble and wavering future plans had firmed suddenly.

He told the Friedmans that he would be leaving for Philadelphia the next day. "I learned on the boat," he said, "that there will be a large meeting of colored folks in Philadelphia on the first of August. I reckon that will be a fine time to find someone who may know my family."

"But," said Mrs. Friedman bluntly, "you do not even know the name of your *mutter. Mein Gott!*"

"I know her first name," said Peter. "Sidney. That is not like looking for a Mary or a Betty. Could be there is not so many old colored ladies name of Sidney in the city of Philadelphia."

Mrs. Friedman nodded, but she did not seem in the least convinced.

Levi Friedman said, "Peter, how important is it that you leave here tomorrow?"

"If I don't," he said, "I will not get to Philadelphia in time for the big meeting of colored folks."

"What kind of a meeting is it?" asked Isaac. "A church meeting?"

"Don't rightly know," Peter said. "One of the barbers on board *The Greek Slave* told me about it. He said I could maybe find out something there about my family."

Isaac nodded. Then he said, "You don't think you should stay here till we've gone to the mayor of Cincinnati—till you have your official free papers?"

"How long would it take me to get these papers?" Peter asked.

"A week or more," said Levi Friedman.

"And how long you planning to stay on in Cincinnati, Mr. Isaac?"

"A month, or more," Isaac Friedman said.

"Then," said Peter, "I could go to Philadelphia for the colored folks' meeting on the first of August. And come back to Cincinnati to have the papers signed. I'd be back well before you leave for the South, Mr. Isaac."

"It's what might happen in between that worries me," said Levi Friedman. "I'm referring to the slave-catchers. They're diligent, for one good reason. They're paid a handsome fee for their troubles."

Peter had heard many dire tales about these slave-catchers. White men down South were fond of repeating all manner of gruesome stories about slave-catchers who roamed the Northern states hunting for runaways. And abolitionists! They, Peter had often been told, were even worse. Over and over he had heard the words, like a refrain: "The abolitionists kidnap niggers and cut off their heads with a meat ax."

It would be far safer, of course, to stay in Cincinnati, have his papers signed by the mayor, and then proceed to Philadelphia and start his search. On the other hand, if he missed the meeting of colored folks in Philadelphia, he might be missing the one clue that could lead him to his parents, his background, his birthplace.

"I—got this feeling strong inside me to go there," he said.

"Then you must go," said Isaac. "But take care, that's all."

"And," Levi added, "don't trust every colored man you meet. Slave-catchers often hire colored agents!"

The next morning, Peter boarded the boat that would take him to Pittsburgh. From there he would take a stagecoach across the Allegheny Mountains to a train, which would carry him to Philadelphia. If he made all his connections, he would arrive in Philadelphia on August 1.

The two Friedman brothers came down to the wharf to see him off. But when their figures had blended into the massed shape of the crowd on shore, and when the outlines of the city had disappeared, curtained by hazy clouds, Peter began to feel fearful.

On the steamship from Tuscumbia he had seen very little of Isaac Friedman. But the knowledge that the man was there was reassurance in itself. Now he was totally alone. The boat that chugged slowly up the Ohio River seemed to be pulling him away from all that he knew and all whom he loved. He felt like jumping overboard and swimming back to the Cincinnati wharf.

He noticed then that a short, dark-haired white man kept staring at him. This same man had attempted several times to draw him into conversation on *The Greek Slave*. Now he gave Peter a sour smile and ambled over to him.

"Is your owner still on board?" he asked.

"I have no owner," said Peter, and walked away.

Some time later an elderly gentleman, very well dressed, came up to him and asked whether his master were on board.

"I have no master," said Peter. "Who said I had a master?"

"But you are a slave," the gentleman persisted. "Or at least you have been one. I knew it as soon as I saw you. Where are you going?"

"To Pittsburgh," said Peter forcefully, "And then to Philadelphia. And I am a free man. Who said I had a master?"

Instead of answering the question, the gentleman asked another. "Where did you come from?"

"From Cincinnati!" said Peter.

He went down to the barber shop, which was empty save for two black barbers. One of them warned Peter that the short, dark-haired man was watching him closely and was whispering to other passengers that Peter was a runaway slave. The man had said these very words while sitting in the barber chair.

Were these two barbers agents for the white man? Suddenly everyone on this boat, black and white, seemed an enemy. Would they arrest him and put him in chains? On a boat there was nowhere to run, and nowhere to hide; there was no escape.

Fear mounted to paralyzing terror.

The calliope was playing on the top deck. The boat was docking at a river port. Should he run off, run away? Where was this place?

A young white man with a pleasant face stopped by Peter as he stood leaning on the railing. "Now, my friend," said the man, speaking softly, "there are a great many watching you, and if you are free, stand to it. Don't leave the boat. Just say that you are free."

Someone else approached, and the young man quickly walked away. Had it been a trick? Should he follow the young man's advice, or do the opposite?

Soon another man was by his side. He wore a broad-brimmed white hat and a scrawny black necktie. "See here, my friend," said he, "people tell me that you are running away. Here is five dollars. If you get off in Wheeling, don't stop there, for they talk of taking you up. And they can do so, for West Virginia's a slave state. Take this five dollars and walk across the bridge. You'll be in a free state, where they can't hurt you."

It was a nightmare boat. He had boarded it in a free state, and it had carried him back to a slave state!

"Take this five dollars," the man said again, holding out a gold piece.

Despite the terror that seemed to clench like a fist at his throat, Peter managed to answer the man. "No, sir, I thank you," he said. "I have paid my passage to Pittsburgh, and I shall not leave the boat. Let them take me up if they like; I can telegraph to my friends in Cincinnati, and I reckon *they* can make 'em pay for the time I'm hindered. Yes; let them take me up if they think best."

The man merely nodded and walked away.

*I done right*, Peter told himself firmly, as his panic mounted. But had he? If he left the boat and ran for the bridge to the free state, they would have good reason to think him a runaway. But if he did not run, he might be arrested when they docked in this slave state. Arrested, and brought back to the Deep South in chains.

# 17

He remained on the boat. He was not arrested, though groups of men watched him constantly and whispered together. He tried to look at them with indifference. And when the boat arrived in Pittsburgh early the next morning, he strapped his small trunk to his back and walked slowly down the gangplank as though he knew exactly where he was going, and why.

The wharf was crowded with color, sound, motion, commotion. Men, horses, mules, carriages, carts; boats unloading, passengers boarding. Every variety of vessel seemed to converge on the harbor: paddle-wheelers, flatboats, ferries, sailboats, rowboats, barges. Thankful for the cover of confusion, Peter hurried along the wharf and ducked down a narrow side street. It stank of sewage and manure. He glanced behind him. No one seemed to be following him, yet he felt pursued. He ran into another street, and was stopped short by a group of grunting pigs.

He finally came to a street that was broader, free of pigs, and filled with people. He knew that he had to leave Pittsburgh by stagecoach. But where was the coach stop? He was afraid to ask. Was Pittsburgh slave territory, or free? Would he be arrested here? Why had he not remained in Cincinnati, where he was safe!

He saw a black porter wheeling bricks in a barrow. When Peter asked the way to the stagecoach stop, the man said it would be simpler to show him than to explain. So Peter loaded his trunk onto the bricks, took both handles of the barrow, and followed his guide to the stage stop. He reflected that anyone seeing him would not think he had come very far since his days in the Lexington brickyard when he had wheeled bricks in a barrow at the age of nine.

He waited at the stop for five hours.

From where he sat, Pittsburgh looked like a fine and beautiful city, far larger even than Cincinnati. But he had no wish to explore the place. He feared he might get lost and miss the coach. And somehow he felt that he would not be safe from arrest until he was in the city of Philadelphia.

The coach, when it finally came, was crowded. He had paid for a seat inside but was asked to sit up with the black driver. When they came to the mountains he was glad to be outside.

"They're called the Alleghenies," the driver told him, and Peter was spellbound by the awesome, ever-changing beauty. Soaring peaks, stretching hemlocks, hillsides flecked with the brightness of wildflowers. The grandeur of the scenery made him feel small sometimes, and sometimes soaring. He wished fervently that Vina were here beside him as the stagecoach clattered over the road that wound through these wild, rough mountains.

They stopped for the night at a roadside inn. Peter shared a small room above the stable with the coach driver, who immediately fell onto the bed and dropped off into a deep, snoring sleep. Peter, however, lay staring up into the darkness, his thoughts pervaded by fears and by memories.

He missed Vina so intensely that he went to his trunk and took out a gingham cape and a patched, threadbare skirt she had given him during their last hour together. "When you want to see something of me," she told him, "you can look at these. They'll make you think of Vina."

He pressed his face into the clothing, remembering the torn sound of her weeping as she and Catharine stood in the doorway of the cabin watching him walk away. And he used Vina's gingham cape to wipe his own tears.

He, a fifty-year-old man, had cried more since he had his freedom than during his whole adult life.

He remembered his stern words to his children on that last Sunday together. "Do not marry till you hear from me, for if I live, I will get you out sure." And he remembered the pained look on the face of his young son, Peter. He was asking the boy to give up the only real happiness a slave could know.

It was cruel, and it was crazy. He could never get them out. What did freedom mean, except enforced separation from his family? He had heard many tales of the terrible hardships endured by "free niggers" who had no one to house, feed, clothe, and look after them. Peter had always tried to discount these stories, which, he was convinced, were made up by slave-owners in an attempt to keep "*their* niggers" contented with their lot. But now, suddenly, in this stopover spot on the way to the city he had dreamed of since boyhood, he was certain that all the stories were true. If a stagecoach had come traveling the other way, traveling back home, he would have taken it.

But the coach that stood waiting for its passengers at six the next morning was headed for the train, which would, according to Peter's ticket, deposit him at the railroad station in Philadelphia on the morning of August 1.

As he boarded ths train, Peter's hopes rose on a new spurt of excitement. The only railroad he had ever seen was the one that ran from Muscle Shoals through Decatur and

Tuscumbia. The train jolted into town once a day: two or three rickety little cars, loaded with freight and pulled by a wheezing old locomotive. If there were passengers aboard, the cars would be drawn instead by two or three horses or mules, for the locomotive was given to explosions that made the trip perilous for human cargo.

But the train he boarded now had a long, sleek, shiny black locomotive, which emitted a proud stream of smoke and shrill whistles. And there were eight elegantly furnished railroad cars. It was like sitting on a sofa looking out the window at an ever-changing view. The tracks were smooth and level. The train barely jounced at all as they rolled past villages, fertile farmlands, and fine farmhouses with great stone-based barns.

By the time the train pulled into the station at Philadelphia, Peter felt so elated that he didn't trouble to descend the small iron steps. He jumped straight down to the ground. The baggage was being unloaded from a special car. He retrieved his trunk. And then he stood, looking around, an amazed spectator of the noisy scene.

He had never before seen such a swarm of people. There were men in all manner of clothing, from elegant top hats and frock coats to shabby work clothes. Women swept by in dresses more splendid and stylish-looking than any he had seen down South.

He was in Philadelphia! The very fact that he stood here at last was proof enough that he had it within him to make miracles happen. *Phil-a-del-fee-yah*: the name of the city taught to him by Mother Grace when he was six years old. The name of the city he had carried with him like a hope and beacon promising the way to a future as a free man.

Philadelphia. He knew very well it was a name Mother Grace had dredged from her memory, merely because it was a city on the Delaware. But the shack he and Levin

*145*

were stolen from *had* been near the Delaware. Perhaps the old lady had guessed correctly. Perhaps he would learn, here in Philadelphia, who he was, where he had come from, and whether he had living relatives here in the North—relatives who might help him free Vina and the children from bondage.

For the first time since leaving home, he felt confidence, and pride that he had come this far.

The station crowd began to scatter. Friends met friends and quickly departed. Everyone seemed in a hurry. Only he, Peter, stood alone.

He had been advised by the stagecoach driver to go to a certain boardinghouse run by a Negro preacher named Dr. Byas. But the driver had given him no address. How to find one small boardinghouse in this vast city?

The warnings began to come back to him, and the fears aroused by the white men on the boat. *Suppose*, he thought to himself, *some abolitionist should come along now, mighty friendly, and tell me where to go, and I should be trapped and sold again!*

After he had stood alone for more than half an hour an elderly black man came up to him and said, "Do you wish to go to some part of the city, friend?"

For a moment Peter did not answer. Levi Friedman had warned him that slave-hunters often employed colored agents to lure prospects into a trap. On the other hand, how long could he stand here on the empty platform? "I was recommended to a boardinghouse, kept by a preacher named Dr. Byas," Peter said.

"Well," said the stranger, "I know where he lives, and I will carry your trunk there for a quarter."

Peter nodded. And the old man hoisted the trunk onto his shoulders and led the way.

They entered the city, which, his guide informed him,

was the second biggest in the United States. "They say that half a million people live here," the old man commented chattily. "They call this the city of Brotherly Love, did you know that, friend?"

"It sure is a city of plenty carriages," Peter said. They cluttered the streets: carriages and carts of all sizes and shapes clattered over the cobblestones. The streets, he noted, ran in straight lines. They were far cleaner than those he had seen in Cincinnati or Pittsburgh. The buildings were chiefly of brick, smooth and fine and neatly laid. Perhaps he could find work here in a brickyard.

The pavements were made of granite, and they, like the streets, were swept clean. The shops had brightly colored awnings out front, and behind the plate-glass windows were views of elegant counters and shelves displaying wondrous wares.

Now that he was here, walking through the tree-shaded streets, he found Philadelphia even more beautiful than anything he had imagined.

But when they entered the colored section, the dream city vanished. Many of the houses were squalid. The wooden buildings looked as though they were on the point of collapse. The streets stank of garbage.

"Do you know where the meeting of colored folks will be held?" Peter asked.

"Which meeting?" said the old man, and he spat out a stream of tobacco juice.

"Why—the big meeting. The August first meeting. Colored folks come into the city from all over the countryside?"

"Never heard of no such meeting," the old man said.

"Yes!" Peter cried. "There is such a meeting! I heard about it way back on the riverboat. Before I even reached Cincinnati."

"Well," the old man chuckled, "then you just better get

back on that riverboat and ask *them* where the meeting is at!"

Suddenly Peter knew. This old man was an agent, a spy. Leading him straight to an abolitionist's den.

"Well, this here's the place. The Byas boardinghouse." The old man stopped before a three-story brick building. "You want me to carry your trunk up to your room?"

"No," said Peter, "thank you for your trouble." He paid the man, who touched his cap and walked away.

Should he, Peter, do the same? Walk—run—from this place? But where would he run to? He was tired, thirsty, hungry, and his trunk was heavy.

He mounted the steps and lifted the heavy brass door knocker.

Presently a mulatto woman opened the door. She had a pleasant face and a kind smile. "Yes?" she inquired.

"Excuse me, ma'am," said Peter. "I was told there was a big meeting of colored folks in Philadelphia today."

She looked puzzled. "Church meetings, that's all. Nothing big—not that I've heard of."

He nodded. It was all a trick, a trap. The net of agents was spread from here to the riverboat. Get him to Philadelphia without his official papers. Then we can lock him up, chain him, send him back South. And collect a big fee for tracking down a runaway slave. He still *was* a slave in Alabama. Mr. Isaac had explained that to him clear enough. A slave who belonged to no one—not even to himself.

"I'm Mrs. Byas," the woman said. "Would you like to come in for a spell? Sit down? Maybe I can find someone who knows about the big meeting."

Because he did not know where else to go or what else to do, he followed her inside. She led him to the parlor, which was comfortably furnished. Soft sunlight filtered through the lace curtains at the window.

"Have a seat," she said.

But he did not sit down. Instead, he abruptly asked her, "Do you know how far it is to the Delaware River?"

"Why, yes," she said. "It's right down this street. At the wharf."

"Well!" he exclaimed, forgetting abolitionists—forgetting everything—"that is just the river I'm hunting for! I was born on that river. And I want to go down now and find the house where my father and mother lived—right on the side of the hill!"

Mrs. Byas looked rather startled. Swiftly Peter told her his story. The kidnaping. The years of slavery. The years of struggle and saving to buy himself.

"I will help you," Mrs. Byas said when he had finished speaking. There were tears in her eyes, and determination in her voice.

She insisted that he come into the kitchen. She fed him lunch. Then she wrote down the street and number of her boardinghouse so that he could find his way back again. He had never before seen a black woman who could write. "We have an empty room," she told him. "Why don't you stay here tonight? After you return from your search of the Delaware."

He nodded agreement, convinced now that Mrs. Byas was a friend. Then he started down to the Delaware.

On his way to the river, he looked into the face of every black man he met, hoping to find some resemblance to himself or to Levin. And when he reached the Delaware, he walked on and on, for miles, looking for the familiar cabin, knowing that the quest was hopeless. But perhaps, just a little farther on. . . .

He walked past the frontage of wooden wharves jutting into the broad river . . . past the huddle of masts and cordage of vessels, the puffing of steamers arriving and departing, the struggling of draymen, porters, and sailors loading and unloading cargo . . . past mountainous piles of coal brought down by railroad to the quay. . . . On he walked, and on, trying to find the outskirts of this city which stretched so far along the Delaware. Nothing was familiar. Even when the dense city lay behind him, the riverbanks were dotted only with the stately dwellings of the rich. He saw not a single wooden cabin that matched the one in his memories.

Finally, with aching feet and aching spirits, he doubled back the way he had come. And by evening he found the boardinghouse of Dr. Byas.

Mrs. Byas did not seem surprised at the outcome of his search. "Even if the cabin was there once," she told him, "you can't expect that the same wooden shack would still be sitting there, waiting for you to find it after more than forty years."

Peter nodded, too dispirited to speak.

"But," Mrs. Byas went on, "you mustn't give up. You've come all this way, you've got to keep trying. Tomorrow I'll send old Ben out with you. He knows lots of the old men and women hereabouts. You can ask them if anyone's heard of a man named Levin and his wife, Sidney, who lost two children all that time ago."

"Do you think there's any hope?" Peter asked.

"There's hope just as long as you keep trying," Mrs. Byas said.

# 18

The following afternoon he returned to the Byas boarding house not only discouraged, but once again fearful.

Ben had indeed taken him to visit elderly colored people of the district. But often Ben would draw someone aside; they would whisper while they cast odd glances at Peter. No one had heard of a couple named Sidney and Levin who had lost two little boys some forty years ago. But Peter began to feel himself sinking into a morass of other people's horror stories. Each person he spoke to seemed to feel he had to outdo Peter's tale with one of his own. One old man who had lived in Philadelphia fifty-three years told him that he knew of sixty children who had mysteriously disappeared from the district in one year. In another year, forty were carried off. No trace was ever found of any of them.

What hope could he, Peter, have of finding his past, and of finding hope and help for his future, when he was a single, floundering ex-slave among so many?

Yet, when he returned to the boardinghouse, Mrs. Byas had thought of another way to help him.

"There's an Anti-Slavery Office on North Fifth Street. They keep records of old colored churches. Since you told me your parents were at church the day you were stolen, they must have been religious people."

"Yes!" Peter cried, "seems to me like I remember now—

my daddy was the one with the keys to the church! A little white wooden church, back off the road. In the woods."

"Well!" Mrs. Byas exclaimed, as though his parents had already been found. "That makes it sure then! Your daddy's name *must* have been on the church register."

Without even stopping for a cup of hot tea, he went off again, accompanied once more by Ben—for Mrs. Byas assured him he would never find North Fifth Street without a guide.

Evening was sifting over the city by the time they reached the Anti-Slavery Office. Peter peered in the window and saw a young man at a desk, writing.

"You ever see a black man doing that in the South?" Ben asked.

"No, indeed," Peter replied. "If a black man there knowed how to write, he'd best keep it a secret."

They entered the office. The clerk was alone. He stood up, smiled, and came toward them. He was handsome, Peter noted, and neatly dressed.

"Good evening, sir," said Ben. "Here is a man from the South who is hunting for his people. He says he was born in Philadelphia. Mrs. Byas thought possibly you might find the name of his parents on some of your books."

The clerk nodded and asked Peter to have a seat.

Then Ben made a small, secretive gesture. But Peter noticed it. Uneasiness seemed to seep through his body as the two men stood by the door talking together. He could hear the soft sound of their words, but not what they were saying.

When the clerk came back to his desk he said to Peter in a businesslike voice, "Now, sir, what were your parents' names?"

The words stumbled out. "I—I was stolen away from the Delaware River when I was six years old."

The clerk nodded again. He stood looking down at Peter.

Presently he said, the words spaced out slowly, "You asked me to search in our records and books for your parents. What were their names?"

Peter swallowed. "My father—his name was Levin. My mother's name was Sidney."

The clerk stared. Then he glanced at Ben, who answered with a small smile.

And suddenly Peter saw the whole scheme. The sign out front—Anti-Slavery Office—was only a lure. This was an abolitionist den! He glanced past the desk, and yes, there in the dimness was another door—a closed door, leading to what? Jail cells inside?

It was clever, indeed. Men came here—confessed their true stories, thinking they were safe in this place, little knowing that a slave-catcher was there in the back room, waiting to arrest them and bring them South in chains.

"Tell me more," the clerk said, speaking very softly now.

Peter stood up.

The clerk glanced at Ben, who seemed to take it as a signal. He ambled to the door, leaned against it.

If he shoved Ben aside, bolted into the street, would they follow him? Throw him down? Drag him back here? He knew he could overpower the slender young clerk and the old man. But who was beyond that door behind the desk? How many? Did they have whips, ropes, dogs?

"Please," the clerk said, "sit down. Tell me more about your family. Tell me all that you remember."

Not knowing what else to do, Peter sat. Not knowing what else to say, he repeated his story.

"One day," he began nervously, "one day when my mother was gone to church, a man came along in a gig, and asked us—"

"Us?" the clerk interrupted sharply. "Who is 'us'?"

"My brother and me."

"What's your brother's name?"

"He is dead now. But he was named after my father."

"Levin?"

Peter nodded.

"Yes?" the clerk said, prodding him to say more.

"This man came along in a gig and asked us if we didn't want to ride. He told us he would carry us to our mother, so we got up with him. But in place of carrying us to our mother, he took us off to Kentucky and sold us. He had no right to sell us." Peter repeated this loudly, so that it could be heard by whoever was listening behind the door. "*He had no right to sell us*. We were free! We came from a free state. My mother and father were not slaves!"

"Are you certain of that?" the clerk said.

"I was told so," said Peter. "In any case, I am free now. I got my certificate of freedom right here. Sewed into my pocket. When I get back to Cincinnati, Mr. Isaac, he'll go with me to the mayor. Then, in a week, I get my printed freedom papers, signed by the mayor of Cincinnati. If you don't believe me, you can send a telegram to Mr. Isaac Friedman. I got his address. He was my master."

He glanced at the window. It was dark outside now. Night had settled into the room. The clerk's face was in shadow. His eyes held flecks of brightness from the yellowish light of the oil lamp. He glanced at Ben and said, "It will take me some time to go through all the old church papers. You may as well leave. I'll see that he gets back to the Byas boardinghouse."

Ben opened the door.

Peter rose hurriedly. "I'll go, too."

"No!" The clerk's voice was sharp. Then it softened. "Please, I promise you, I will do my best to find your family —their records."

"Yes, stay by all means," Ben insisted. "If he'll look through the papers now, you had better stay. That's what you came for, isn't it? I'll tell Mrs. Byas." With a further swift glance at the clerk, he was gone. The door closed behind him with a thud.

"Please," the clerk said. "Sit down. Please. I must ask you a few more questions before we—before we go through the records."

Peter edged toward the door.

"Don't you want to try to find out who you are?" the clerk asked. "Isn't that why you came here?"

"Yes."

"Then sit down. Please."

Peter walked back to the chair and sat. He could not, after all, be certain that this young man was an abolitionist agent.

"Did you have any other brothers?" the clerk asked.

Peter shook his head. "Only Levin. He died in Alabama, nineteen years ago."

"Did you have any sisters?"

"One sister, yes. Mahala. She was older than Levin and me."

There was silence; only a faint hissing sound came from the oil lamp.

Then the clerk said, "That's not a common name, Mahala. Are you certain you remember her name correctly?"

Peter nodded.

"Was there anyone else you remember? Any other member of the family?"

"There was Grandmother."

"Do you remember what they looked like? Your mother or father?"

Peter shook his head. Then he said, "We used to talk a

*155*

heap about our mother, Levin and me. I remember she had a mole on her cheek. But Levin, he claimed it was only a kind of dark spot, not a mole."

"On her cheek," the clerk repeated.

Peter nodded.

Then the clerk said, "Suppose I should tell you that I am your brother?"

Now Peter *knew* that it was a trap. He did not understand quite how he was being tricked, but it was clear that he must proceed carefully.

"My father's name was Levin," the clerk said. "And my mother's name is Sidney. And they lost two boys named Levin and Peter, around the time you speak of. I have often heard my mother mourn about those two children." His voice trembled. "I am sure that you must be one of them."

Peter, of course, did not believe a single word the clerk had said. The man, after all, had done no more than repeat the story he had just heard. But Peter knew now what to do. Pretend. Pretend he believed it all. Make a few easy remarks, to ease his way out of this place.

It was clear what they intended. They thought him some kind of half-wit from the South. They knew he must have money with him. Sooner or later this young man would say: *Since I am your brother, let me keep your money. I'll keep it here safe for you, so you won't get robbed in Philadelphia.*

Trying to keep the fear from his voice, Peter said, "I want to ask you one question: are your father and mother living?"

"My father has been dead for some years," said the clerk. "But my mother is living."

"Well, sir," said Peter, "then your mother is not my mother, for my mother must be dead! My brother said, before he died, that he was sure she was dead; and that is nineteen years ago. Yes, my mother must be dead." He stood up. "I didn't expect to find her alive. But I thought I might find her grave." In a casual way he went toward the door.

But the clerk jumped up, ran to the door, and locked it.

"Look," he said, "I have an older sister who lives nearby. Come with me to see her. She can tell you much more about our family."

Peter nodded. The important thing was to get him to unlock the door. Once they were in the street. . . .

"Her name is Mary," the clerk said. "She teaches school. And she keeps a few boarders. Maybe you'll want to stay with her for the night."

"Maybe," said Peter. Now he understood! This Anti-Slavery Office was only the first step in the trap. This, after all, was a public place. Anyone might walk in at any time, hear the screams from the back, call the police. So they had worked out this smooth system. The victim was lured away in the night. A boardinghouse run by a schoolteacher! With the sweet, saintly name of Mary!

"I know you don't believe me," the clerk said. "But will you come with me to see Mary?"

"Of course!" said Peter.

The clerk unlocked the door. Then he asked, "Do you have a last name?"

Peter relaxed somewhat as they walked out to the street. "My *last* last name was Friedman," he said. "Before that, it was Hogun. Before that, Gist. Before that, Fisher. I had enough of last names. Now, I'm free!"

"You *have* a last name," the clerk said. "A name of your own. The same as mine. My name is William Still. Your name is Peter Still."

Peter nodded.

The clerk looked at him. Then he took out a heavy key and locked the door of the Anti-Slavery Office. They started off down the street. "You don't believe a word of what I'm saying, do you?"

"Of course I believe you," Peter protested. He glanced back. No one was following them. At the next corner he would bolt and run. Hide in the darkness. Then make his way to the railroad station. Anyone could direct him to the railroad station. He would have to leave his trunk behind him. But at least he had his money, all of it; $56, right in his pocket. And his freedom certificate, he had that too. He would make his way back to Cincinnati, and to Isaac Friedman and safety.

"It's not easy to know what to do," the clerk said. "How to feel. What to say, walking down the street with a stranger —who is your brother."

They were at the corner now. But Peter did not run. Instead he stopped, looked at the clerk. The face was masked by darkness. But the way the young man had said those words. . . . What if this were not a trap? What if he had, in fact, met his own younger brother—and ran away?

Suddenly he asked, "Why was that old man Ben whispering to you when he brought me in? What did he say?"

"He said you'd been all over the quarter today, asking questions of everyone. He was certain you were a spy, sent out to hunt for runaways."

"Did *you* think I was a spy?"

"One has to be careful," said William Still.

"And now? What do you think?"

"It seems impossible to believe," said William. "But I am certain that you are my brother."

They started walking again, and Peter decided that he would go and meet the schoolteacher named Mary.

# 19

As Peter sat in the parlor waiting, new fears swept through him.

The woman named Mary had been removing the dinner dishes when they entered. She paid no particular attention to Peter and left him sitting in the musty parlor. William had followed her from the room.

Peter now remembered the chilling stories he had heard about infamous city women who kept houses where strangers were lured to be robbed and sometimes murdered. As a man just come from the South, he would be a fine prospect. They must know he had money sewn into his pocket.

He started to sweat. Was it the heat of the August night, the stuffy parlor? Or was it his own fear?

A gilt-framed mirror hung across from the sofa on which he sat. His reflection was faint in the faded light from the single gas lamp on the wall. He looked like a ghost of himself.

Should he run away? Was the front door locked and bolted?

Just as he got up, the two returned. The woman was carrying a candle in a polished brass holder.

"Sister," said William in a formal manner, "here is a man who tells a strange story. He has come to Philadelphia to look for his relations. And I should like to have you hear what he has to say."

It sounded, thought Peter, like a speech recited many times before. And, as though playing her role, the "sister" sat down and inquired rather stiffly, "For whom are you looking?"

Peter did not want to go through the story again. He merely said, "Oh, I'm looking for a needle in a haystack. And I reckon the needle's rusty and the stack is rotten down. So it's no use to say any more about it."

"*Tell* her!" the clerk said urgently. "Tell her what you told me in the office. Tell her the names of your parents."

"Sidney," he said "was the name of my mother. The name of my father was Levin."

With a scream the woman jumped up, seized her candle, ran to Peter, and held the light near his face. Then she cried. "Oh, Lord, it *is* one of our lost brothers! Thank God! One of our brothers has come!" And she flung both arms around him.

Peter, stunned, tried to free himself, concerned lest her candle should set his shirt on fire.

She released him as suddenly as she had embraced him, and turned to William. "Oh," she wailed. "This will kill Mother! How shall we tell her? The shock will kill her!"

Mary and William decided that the next morning she would bring Peter to their brother James, who lived in New Jersey near their mother. James would know how to break the news to the old lady. He was, after all, a doctor.

A doctor! How could a colored man be a doctor? This, thought Peter, was the final proof he needed. He was trapped like a fly in a sticky web of their lies.

But here, up North, perhaps a black man *could* be a doctor. Maybe he, Peter—cotton-picker, dishwasher, grave-digger—maybe he had a brother who was a doctor!

Mary insisted that he stay the night.

"I cannot," said Peter. "All my things are at the Byas boardinghouse."

"I can give you what you need for the night," Mary told him. "No use to go all the way back there if we're setting off for New Jersey early in the morning."

"I'll stop by the Byas place," said William. "I'll tell Mrs. Byas what's happened, so she won't think you got lost."

Peter shrugged. If all this *was* a plot, Mrs. Byas would be part of it, and he would be no safer in her boardinghouse than in the home of this woman, Mary.

She gave them some dinner, and William left. Then Peter followed his "sister" upstairs.

She threw her arms about him once more and wept a little before she said good night.

Her bursts of emotion served only to assure him that she was play-acting. Alone in the room, he locked the door. Then he went to the window, opened it wide, and peered out into the night. The haze of gas lamps softened the outlines of the city.

His room was high up, on the fourth floor; it was too far to jump should attackers burst in.

Perhaps someone was here already, hiding.

He looked under the bed. Only darkness.

He shoved a heavy chest in front of the door. Then he took off his shoes, folded his jacket carefully, and put it under the bolster; he lay down determined to think out some plan of escape should thieves burst in to rob and murder him.

But he was exhausted from the long day of trekking about, and he fell asleep; fell into a tangle of nightmares. He was in the cabin with Vina and their small children.

McKiernan and the overseer came, chained him up, and dragged him away. . . . He was about to leave Tuscumbia with Isaac Friedman. But he could not go, for during the night someone had stolen all his clothes. . . . Armed men were entering his room, this room!

He startled awake, listened for footsteps. There was only silence.

After a time he fell asleep once more; a sleep still ripped by terrifying dreams.

The next day, however, in the soft sunlight of early morning, his apprehension vanished. As he sat on the small steamboat next to this woman named Mary, he felt a rising excitement. He was certain that she was not his sister. But he was, in any case, embarking on an adventure. And now he was far more ready to cope with whatever might come.

Perhaps the new confidence came from the fact that he was at last on the Delaware River, the only real clue he had to the place of his childhood. The Delaware had been like the polestar of his hopes. And sailing on it affirmed his feeling that good things could happen, could be made to happen—even by a man who had lived his life as a slave.

Mary, who obviously did not doubt that he accepted her as a "long-lost sister," chattered on about "the family."

He and Levin, she claimed, had been born as slaves. They had not been born in or near Philadelphia. Not at all. They were born in northern Maryland, where their parents, Levin and Sidney, were slaves.

Peter looked at her and pretended interest in what she was saying. Maryland! Where was that? He had never even heard of Maryland! What did she know, this stout, chattering, middle-aged lady? He had been born in a free state! He had always known this. And then she told him something that proved she was telling him lies.

After the two little boys were stolen, she said, the father, Levin, had bought his own freedom.

Peter turned to stare at this fat "sister." Did she truly expect him to believe that his daddy, too, had bought his freedom?

First they expected him to accept total strangers as his sister and brother. And now they thought him fool enough to swallow *this* story!

But Mary was chattering on, as though she never sensed his distrust and disbelief.

"Of course, Daddy didn't have to pay much for himself," she explained with a light laugh. "Never would tell us *how* much. But he was young, and his master was young, and he told his master, 'I do not aim to spend my days as a slave.' They lived on the east coast of Maryland. Not that far from New Jersey. And part of New Jersey was free. I suppose the master knew if he *didn't* let Daddy buy himself, he'd have a runaway slave to start looking for."

Peter nodded. "And—Sidney?" he asked flatly. "She buy herself, too, from this master?"

"She *did* run away," said Mary. "Daddy was working in a sawmill in New Jersey. And Mama took us, Mahala and me, to join him. I was only a babe in arms, so I don't remember the running away. But Mahala does. And she remembers the fear. Even when we were safe in a free part of New Jersey, Mama was terrified that we'd be arrested as runaways and carried back to slavery. So she changed her name. She called herself Charity."

*Oh, yes, surely*, said Peter to himself. *Now, suddenly I am on my way to meet an old lady named Charity—not Sidney!*

It was early afternoon when the steamer landed at Long

Bridge. They took seats in the stagecoach for Medford, ten miles away. Then they walked from the coach stop to the home of Dr. James Still, which lay on the main road close by the town.

"You'll be proud to meet your brother James," said Mary. "Dr. James Still."

"Didn't know a black man could be a doctor," Peter remarked.

"That didn't stop James." Mary said. "Nothing," she added, "could stop James."

She told him then the remarkable tale of this "brother," who had been born in New Jersey in a two-room log cabin at Indian Mills in the year 1812. James had never lived a day of his life as a slave. Like the other sons, he had worked his way through childhood. And like them, he'd had a few months of schooling as a small boy.

"But by eighteen," said Mary, "that little bit of learning was long forgotten. He couldn't write. Couldn't do the simplest sums. Yet, he had this thing burning within him: he wanted to be a doctor!"

It was a hot afternoon. Peter wiped his hand over his forehead to keep sweat from dripping down into his eyes. Yet, at the same time, he felt chilled inside. He well understood what it meant to have an impossible hope burning there inside, from boyhood on.

"Then," Mary exclaimed, "at age eighteen James got his chance. He was bound to a farmer named Wilkins for a term of three years, two months, and five days. The payment for this was $100, a new suit of clothes—and three months of schooling, one month each winter!"

Again Peter looked at her, waiting. How far could a man go on three months of schooling?

"He went to Philadelphia," said Mary. "Walked all the

way. Took any kind of job he could get. And he saved money. Saved—and studied. He bought himself three medical books on the stalls in Philadelphia. One on medical botany cost a dollar. Another on anatomy cost a dollar and twenty-five cents."

Three months of schooling and three books. How far could a man go on three medical books?

"Then he went back to New Jersey," said Mary. "Built himself a cabin in the woods. He was married and had a young daughter. And he worked to support them. Worked as a laborer. But he kept on learning. He learned to make medicines from the leaves and roots that he found in the forest. First he used his potions only to heal members of his own family. But neighbors began to hear about him. They came and they begged for his cures. They told others, who came and were cured. Not all were cured, of course—he's not a miracle man. But he has a kind of genius for knowing what to do, how to help." She turned to Peter. "Your brother James is now one of the most respected men in Medford, New Jersey. The countryside is filled with folks who have been cured by Dr. James Still."

They rounded a bend in the road, and Mary pointed. "There it is. James's new house—which he owns."

It was a fine wooden house, painted white, with many glass windows edged by long green shutters.

And the man coming to meet them was his dead brother, Levin!

"James," Mary exclaimed, "I have brought someone to see you."

"What's the trouble, sir?" James said, concerned. "Are you in pain?"

Peter stood there in the roadway, tears streaming down his cheeks.

The same broad forehead, thin face, long nose. . . . His brother Levin . . . his brother James. . . .

He had found his family. He had come home.

They took him to meet his mother. She lived eight miles away. In the carriage, James warned him that the news must come gently. "She could be felled by the shock. She's almost eighty years old, and frail."

Peter understood this well. *He* had been almost felled by the shock of seeing James. And he had been half prepared since the moment William had said: "Suppose I should tell you that I am your brother?"

They drove up to the small farm, which their father had owned and had left to his wife and son Samuel when he died.

She was standing in the front doorway.

Despite all the warnings, Peter's first impulse was to jump from the carriage, run to her, take her into his arms. She did not look familiar. Yet, she was not a stranger—like James, and Mary, and William. He had kept her alive for himself by cherishing the few fragments of memories. Her face had faded from his mind. But now that he saw her, a thin, white-haired old lady in the doorway, he was overcome by all the repressed and remembered emotions.

"Go gently," said James as they walked toward the house. "Very gently."

"Howdy, Mother," Mary said, kissing her.

"Why, what are you doing away out here?" Mrs. Still asked, surprised. "Why aren't you working?"

"It's August, remember?" Mary said. "No school in August."

"Oh, yes. My memory is slipping. Come inside, children." She looked at Peter.

His heart thudded. He *remembered* her face. And there

was the mole, on her left cheek. *Mother*. He forced back the flood of tenderness and smiled politely.

"I've brought someone to meet you," Mary said.

"Always glad to meet friends of my children," the old woman said to Peter. "Come inside, all."

They entered the room, which was neat, scrubbed clean, and simply furnished.

The mother sat in a rocker by the window, and Peter took a chair beside her. "I understand," he said, "that you have many fine children."

"Oh, yes, indeed," she replied. This seemed to be a subject she liked to dwell on. And she told him with pride about the children: the sons, James, John Nelson, Samuel, William; and the girls, Mary, Keturah—whom they called Kitty—and the oldest child, Mahala, who lived nearby.

"Mahala," Peter repeated softly.

"I have had eighteen children," she told him. "I have buried nine, and I have seven living."

Very carefully Peter said, "I thought you said you had eighteen—seven living and nine dead would make but sixteen."

The old woman heaved a sigh. "Ah," she said, "them two boys have been more trouble to me than all the rest of my children. I've grieved about them a good many years."

*Mama!* cried the boy, Peter, inside the man. *We did not forget you! And you did not forget us!*

Quietly he asked, "What became of those two boys?"

"I never knew what became of them. I left them asleep in the bed, the last time I ever saw them. I never knew whether they was stolen, or what happened to them."

Peter looked at Mary imploringly. Was it time now to reveal who he was? And if it was, *he* could not do it. He could not speak.

Mary came to her mother, knelt before her, held her thin

hands. "Mama," she said softly. "He has come back. This is your son, Peter."

The old woman looked at Peter as though she had not heard. Then she rose and walked stiffly into the next room, where she knelt in prayer.

They watched her through the open door. "Should I go to her?" Mary whispered to James. But he shook his head.

In a short time, the old woman got to her feet and returned. She was trembling, but her face was calm. She came to Peter. "Who are you?" she said.

The words came somehow. "My name is Peter. And I had a brother, Levin. My father's name was Levin, and my mother's name was Sidney—"

The mother uttered a cry. "Oh, Lord, how long have I prayed to see my two sons! Can it be that they have come?" She looked at Peter. "Oh, if you are my child, tell me howdy once more!"

His arms went around his mother, and they wept together.

# 20

Peter returned to Philadelphia a week later to find that he had become something of a celebrity. Old Ben, like a town crier, had spread the news. A six-year-old boy, stolen from his home, having no facts about which state he had come from, had, at the age of fifty, walked into the Anti-Slavery Office on North Fifth Street—and found his brother sitting there behind the desk.

Among those who wanted to meet Peter Still was a white man named Seth Conklin, an abolitionist.

During the week in his mother's home, Peter had learned many things—including the fact that abolitionists were not the fearsome, evil demons that white Southerners had portrayed them to be. Quite the contrary. There were white abolitionists who had risked their livelihood and their very lives to help runaway slaves reach the North and freedom.

It now appeared that this Seth Conklin was prepared to do just that for Peter and his family.

Peter and Conklin met one evening in the Anti-Slavery Office. No one was present except William, who introduced the white man and presented the plan.

"Mr. Conklin," said William, "belongs to no official abolitionist society. He doesn't need to." William smiled. "He's a whole society in himself. I won't tell you all that he has done for our cause. The fewer people who know those de-

tails, the better. What matters now, Peter, is what he's prepared to do for *your* cause. And that's why I've asked you
two men to meet here this evening."

Conklin sat leaning back in his chair, legs crossed, smok-
ing a pipe. His dark hair was fringed with gray. There was
nothing of the city man about him; he had the browned and
weathered face of a farmer. As he spoke, outlining his plan,
he became intense. Peter listened, amazed. Conklin was
prepared to travel alone to the McKiernan plantation.
There he would meet Vina in secret and guide her, the two
boys, and Catharine back through the slave states—
Alabama, Tennessee, and Kentucky—to Cincinnati, where
the family would be reunited. It was a distance of some 800
miles. Conklin wanted no payment for this venture: he
asked only enough to cover the expenses of the journey,
perhaps a hundred dollars. And he would need "credentials," something to satisfy Vina that he had, in fact, come
from her husband and was to be trusted.

"Credentials," Peter said, speaking slowly. "I can give
you Vina's own gingham shawl. Money I can get you. I can
find a job, and maybe in a year I can save a hundred dollars. But, sir, if you are asking my permission for this plan
—that I can't give you."

"But why not?" William got up from the desk and came
to his brother. "Peter, do you know how many thousands of
slaves would gladly risk their lives for the chance that Seth
Conklin is offering you?"

"Yes," said Peter, "they *would* risk their lives. And that
is why I can't give permission." He turned to Conklin.
"Since early boyhood, sir, I have heard tales of what happens to runaways who are caught. I have seen women
whipped almost to death. I have seen men and women dragging through the cotton fields week after week in clanking

*170*

chains. No one in the South would treat a dog the way they treat a runaway slave."

"Yes," said Conklin, "a slave who is caught. It is not my intention that we get caught."

"No runaway," said Peter, "has the intention of being caught. You, yourself, sir, if you were caught—they might kill you."

"I'm aware of that," said Conklin.

"Then *why?*" Peter asked, leaning forward, straining to understand this man. "Why do you offer to do this thing? And why for me—why not for one of the thousands of others?"

"Because," Seth Conklin exhaled the pipe smoke slowly, "because of what you have already done for yourself."

"I never risked chains," said Peter. "Or dogs set after me. Or death. I saved the money to buy myself. I can save the money to buy my wife. Then Vina and I can work—and buy our children."

"Two questions," said William sharply. "How long did it take you to save the money to buy yourself? And what makes you think McKiernan would sell Vina—to you?"

"I can earn money easier up North," said Peter. "Maybe my new brothers and sisters will help me out some. They said they would. And maybe Mr. Isaac Friedman would buy Vina, like he bought me. And give *her* a certificate of freedom."

"I know enough about the dear old Southland," said Conklin, "to suspect that your friend, Mr. Friedman, won't thrive very well in Tuscumbia if it becomes known that he buys slaves in order to give them their freedom."

Peter had to agree. It was possible that people would believe that *he* had run away from his master, Friedman the Jew. But if Friedman then offered to buy Vina, everyone would suspect that he planned to let *her* "escape" too. And McKiernan would not sell.

"In a few months," William said, speaking gently now, "your wife and children could be with you. You've seen your family here in the North. We all work hard—but at jobs we have chosen. Most of us own our own homes. Our children have all been educated. Your children can get on in the same way, if they have the same chance. Mr. Conklin is offering them that chance. Now. Instead of your waiting for years and years and years. And for what? For their owner to take your money—and refuse to release his slaves."

Peter said nothing. He stood up and walked to the window. But it was black outside; there was nothing to see. There was a poster on the wall; he went over to it, but he could not read the words that were written there.

Finally he turned to Conklin and said, "If you are willing to risk your life, sir—then I must be willing to risk the lives of Vina and my two boys and my girl."

It was settled then, swiftly. Peter would return to Cincinnati, where Mr. Isaac Friedman had promised to get him his official free papers and a job. He would work to save the money Seth Conklin needed for the expedition. Meanwhile, said William, the family would contribute to his fund as much as they could. As soon as sufficient money had been collected, Conklin would leave for the South.

Two weeks later, on the twenty-second day of August, 1850, Peter Still and Isaac Friedman left the office of H. E. Spencer, Mayor of the City of Cincinnati.

Peter held a long, hand-written document. It had been penned with great care by the mayor's secretary, a pale, bony young man who wore spectacles.

When they left the building, Peter said, "Would you read this to me, Mr. Friedman?"

Isaac Friedman answered, "I would be honored, Mr. Still."

Standing on the sidewalk under a shade tree, as passersby glanced at them curiously, Isaac Friedman slowly and clearly read the words that guaranteed Peter Still was henceforth and forever a free man:

"State of Ohio, } *ss.*
City of Cincinnati. }

Be it known that before me, Henry E. Spencer, Mayor of said City, personally appeared Isaac S. Friedman, who being duly sworn, deposes and says: that he has been acquainted with a colored man named Peter Still, alias Peter Friedman, for the last five years: that the said Peter was formerly a slave belonging to John H. Hogun, residing about three miles from Tuscumbia, in the State of Alabama: that Joseph Friedman, of Tuscumbia, hired the said Peter for about two years of the said John H. Hogun, and afterwards bought him, and held him as a slave for about two years longer, when Peter bought his freedom from his master, the said Joseph Friedman, brother of this deponent, by paying him the sum of five hundred dollars; as fully appears from a bill of sale given by said Joseph Friedman to said Peter, and dated Tuscumbia, Ala., the 16th day of April, 1850, which bill of sale this deponent fully recognizes as genuine.

And further this deponent sayeth not.

ISAAC S. FRIEDMAN."

"The foregoing affidavit of the above-named Isaac S. Friedman, to the freedom of the within-named Peter Still, having been duly sworn to and subscribed before me,—

I therefore do declare the above-named Peter Still, alias Peter Friedman, to be a free person, and entitled to all the privileges of free persons of color, according to the laws of the State of Ohio.

Said Peter Still is about forty-nine years of age, is five feet seven and a half inches in height, of a brownish black complexion, and without any marks or cuts.

Given under my hand, and the Corporate Seal of the City of Cincinnati, this 22d day of August, 1850.

H. E. SPENCER,
Mayor."

Five months later, Seth Conklin set off for the South.

Peter had found a job as a carriage driver in Cincinnati. His mistress was kind. His quarters were comfortable. The pay was sufficient, and by saving all of it and taking on extra work on his time off, he managed to amass almost $60, which he gave to Conklin for the trip, along with Vina's gingham cape.

Then Peter lived like a man treading water—until the promised letter came from a "Mr. Miller," which was the name under which Conklin had chosen to travel.

Isaac Friedman had left Cincinnati, so Peter brought his letter to Levi Friedman and asked him to read it aloud.

First, however, Levi read the letter to himself, and frowned.

Peter sat stiffly, waiting, afraid.

"Well," Levi said at last, "he explains that his first object was to explore the route, discover safe hiding places, and—as he puts it—'to ascertain who in the border free states would be willing to befriend and aid me when I come there with my protégées. . . . However, it seems that the southern boundaries of Illinois and Indiana—free states—are infested with men thirsting for the rewards offered to those who are willing to cast aside their humanity and do the work of bloodhounds, hunting the outcast and seeking and dragging back the fugitive. Searching the country opposite Paducah, Kentucky, I found the whole country, fifty miles around, is inhabited by Christian wolves. It is customary, when a strange Negro is seen, for any white man to seize him and convey him through and out of the state of Illinois to Paducah, and lodge such stranger in Paducah jail, and then claim such reward as may be offered by the master.' "

Friedman stopped reading. He looked up.

Peter's expression was grim. "Even in a free state, they're not safe. They can still be sent back."

"So it seems," said Levi Friedman. "Your Mr. Conklin found no friends on the borders of Illinois. But he writes that, 'trusting nevertheless to a good Providence, I plan to cross to Paducah, and take a steamboat on the Tennessee River for South Florence, Alabama.' "

"South Florence!" Peter exclaimed. His heart started thudding. South Florence was the river town closest to Mc-Kiernan's plantation.

"What is the date of that letter?" he asked.

"It was mailed," said Friedman, "on February 3."

"He must be with my Vina now." Peter closed his eyes in a wordless prayer. "Right this same minute, they may all be heading North."

He lived through another agonizing month, hearing nothing. Then a second letter came.

Once again Peter brought it to Levi Friedman. This time Friedman scanned it and gave a shout.

"*What?*" cried Peter.

"Listen to this! On Saturday night—the first Saturday night in March—they all got passes. For South Florence. Conklin was waiting at the river. At three in the morning, they got into the skiff and rowed all night. They reached Eastport by daylight. And they passed a steamboat. Your son Levin called to the others to lie flat on the bottom of the skiff. Only Conklin was to keep rowing."

"But *why?*"

"Because Levin had recognized one of the steamboat passengers leaning on the railing, looking out. It was Mc-Kiernan."

"Oh!"

"But he didn't see them," said Levi. "Let us hope this means Providence is sailing with them."

"Amen," Peter said.

Friedman then read directly from "Mr. Miller's" letter: " 'During Sunday we were hailed once by half a dozen men on shore, to know where we were from, where going, etc. There being a strong head wind, I appeared as if I could not hear them. I know not what they would have done if they had had a good skiff. . . . I had previously informed myself of the scarcity of good skiffs on the Tennessee River, on which thing alone rested a part of our safety.

" 'I stood at the helm whenever we were in sight of anybody, keeping Levin and Peter at the oars. At all other times, and during the nights, I was principally at the oars. In the daytime I caused Vina and Catharine to lie under the blankets, so as not to be seen. They had a hard time of it. Having a strong head wind, the water dashed into the boat, so as to keep the blankets all the time wet. . . .

" 'At five o'clock, Monday evening, for the first time, I lay down under a blanket. . . . The boys said two men were calling to us in a skiff near the shore, and coming toward us. I ordered that no effort should be made to run. The two men came alongside, demanding where we were going, and "whar from? Are you all black men aboard?" The boys replied in Southern phrase, "White Massa lyin' thar, sir."

" 'When I arose on my knees, partly throwing off my blankets and staring my assailants in the face, they bowed, with "How de do, sir," . . . gave my boat a scrutinizing look, and retired.' "

Peter sighed with relief. And Levi Friedman continued, " 'During Monday night a squall of wind came near dashing our craft to pieces against the large trees. But we succeeded in getting between the trees to the shore, and there remained one hour before we could start. Arrived on the Ohio at sunrise Tuesday morning—fifty-one hours' time. It should have been done, under favorable circumstances, in thirty-six hours. The current of the Tennessee is very stiff. On the Ohio I intended to travel exclusively at nights. Circumstances were against me, and I was compelled to travel as much by day as by night. One half of two nights it was so dark that I could not navigate. . . . I had no fair wind from the time I started till I arrived at Harmony. It would be impossible to describe the difficulties encountered.' "

"Harmony!" said Peter sharply. "Where is that place?"

"This letter is postmarked," said Levi Friedman, "New Harmony, Indiana."

"Indiana!" Peter cried out. "A free state!"

"Indiana," Friedman repeated. "A free state. The letter is dated March 23. Your family may very soon be arriving in Cincinnati."

But the days dragged by, and there was no word.

The days became weeks, and there was no word.

Peter's family had been on free soil since March 23. Yet, by May 23 there was still no word.

Finally, on the last day of May, a telegram arrived from his sister Mary: CAN YOU COME TO PHILADELPHIA.

Were they there? His wife, his sons, his daughter? Would they be waiting in Mary's house to surprise him?

Why had the telegram not been sent by "Mr. Miller"?

177

Why hadn't Conklin brought them to Cincinnati, as planned?

Peter left at once for the train station.

Mary was alone in the parlor. He saw her reflection in the mirror. She was sewing.

He stood in the doorway, afraid to enter. "What has happened?" he said stiffly.

She cried out, startled. Then she rose. "I didn't hear you come in. Did you knock? Did the girl open the door?"

"What has happened?" Peter said again.

"Come in. Sit down."

He sat on the red plush sofa. "Please—what has happened?"

She went to the desk, took out a newspaper clipping, handed it to him.

Peter looked down at it. He could read only the date: *Thursday morning, May 29, 1851*. Then he said, still staring at the newspaper, "Don't you know that I can't read?"

"They were—taken," Mary said. "Conklin is dead."

"And my family?"

"There is only one line about your family. It says, 'The slaves went back to bondage.'"

"The slaves went back to bondage."

"I am so sorry," Mary said.

"Would you read me all of the article?"

She took the newspaper from him and read slowly:

"A SINGULAR ENTERPRISE.—During the last trip of the steamer *Paul Anderson*, Captain Gray, she took on board, at Evansville, Indiana, a United States Marshal, having in custody an intelligent white man, named J. H. Miller, and a family of four slaves—mother, daughter, and two sons. Captain Gray subsequently learned from Mrs. Miller that

*178*

he had been employed by some persons in Cincinnati to go to Florence, Alabama, and bring away this family of slaves—the woman's husband being in a free State. For this purpose, with a six-oared barge, procured at Cincinnati, Miller had gone down the Ohio and up the Tennessee River, to Florence, there laid in wait till an opportunity occurred, and privily taken away the family of slaves. The barge was rowed down the Tennessee, and up the Ohio, to the Wabash, and up that river till within thirty miles of Vincennes, where the party was overtaken and captured by the Marshal. The unfortunate Miller was then chained, to be taken back to Florence for trial and sure condemnation, by Alabama slave laws. The *Paul Anderson* having landed at Smithland, mouth of Cumberland River, Mr. Miller made an attempt to escape from her to the steamer *Mohican*, lying alongside, but, encumbered by his manacles and clothing, was drowned. The body was recovered and buried about a week afterwards. The slaves went back to bondage. The barge was rowed down the Tennessee 273 miles, up the Ohio 100 miles, and up the Wabash 50 miles, before the party were overtaken. Mr. Miller, we learn, had a sister and other relatives in or near Philadelphia. He was a mill-wright by occupation, and owned property in the neighborhood of Vincennes."

When she had finished reading she said, "This was printed in a newspaper in Pittsburgh. Someone sent it to William. It was William who asked me to tell you what happened. He did not know how."

"It is just what I expected," Peter said.

# 21

He returned to Cincinnati. The Friedman family had helped him before. Now, somehow, they would help him again; they must help him again.

Staring out of the train window, he saw springtime. Saw soft blue sky over greening fields. Saw farmers plowing behind horses and oxen. Saw children playing, running through the sunshine. He saw these things with his eyes. But the dark visions he saw in his mind were far more vivid: visions of torture and death, which *he* had brought on his family—by agreeing to Conklin's plan.

He remembered Mary, a beautiful woman, one of McKiernan's favorites. Because of this, she had been the victim of unbearable beatings by Mrs. McKiernan. Mary had run away. When she was found and brought in she was beaten cruelly. After that she was stripped and beaten daily, until she became so weak that McKiernan feared she would be "ruined." So they stopped the beatings. A heavy log-chain was welded to an iron band around her ankle, brought up, and locked around her waist. Month after month she was forced to wear the irons. Peter had often seen her on Sundays when he came to visit. The once proud and beautiful woman was ragged and dirty. She had, Vina told him, "no spirit left to wash and mend her clothes." He had heard the clanking of her heavy chains as she walked through the slave quarters. The clacking of train wheels on the track was magnified into clanking chains, and the image of this tortured woman would not leave his mind. But now the woman was Vina.

And Catharine? And his sons, Peter and Levin . . . ?

He remembered a runaway boy who had been locked to the plow by his chains. The sweat beneath the iron collar had rubbed his skin raw. But his master swore he should wear the collar until he died. And within a few weeks, the threat was fulfilled. The flesh had rotted under the iron collar—which was still around his neck when the young slave died.

McKiernan was known by his slaves as one of the most evil masters in the county. What chance, what hope did Vina and Catharine, Peter and Levin, have now?

Their only hope lay with Isaac Friedman, their only white friend in the South.

When Levi Friedman read the clipping Peter had handed him, his face paled. "Conklin—dead!"

Peter nodded.

"And your family? Any word from them?"

Peter's voice was hoarse with anguish. " 'The slaves went back to bondage!' That is all I know."

Levi Friedman at once sent a telegram to his brother in Tuscumbia. It was a coded message: ANY NEWS OF THE STILLMAN FAMILY? "Stillman," said Levi, "will sound as though one Jew is inquiring about another. The telegraph operator in Tuscumbia won't know that your second name is Still."

There was no answer to the telegram.

"Perhaps it never got there," said Levi, and he promised

Peter that he would go himself to Tuscumbia to learn the fate of the captured runaways.

He began to make preparations for his journey South. Then a letter arrived for Levi from a Mr. Thornton in Tuscumbia, a young man who taught in the boys' school in town. He was, he said, Isaac Friedman's friend.

He wrote that when McKiernan's runaways were brought back on *The Greek Slave*, the people of Tuscumbia had turned in fury against Friedman. They called him a vile abolitionist. They were sure it was he who had planned the escape of Peter's family!

Thornton had warned Isaac Friedman to leave town at once, for his life was in peril. Friedman had taken the warning and was now on his way to Illinois. On no account, the letter concluded, should Levi Friedman think of coming to Tuscumbia. "To do so," wrote Thornton, "would be both hazardous and futile."

"I could go there using another name," Friedman suggested.

Peter shook his head. "You would have to use another face. You look just like your brother." Suddenly Peter said, "Will you write, sir, and ask Mr. Thornton if he will see whether my family are dead or alive? And if they are alive, will he ask Mr. McKiernan whether or not he will sell them to me? And, if he will, at what price?"

Friedman stared. "What could make you imagine, Peter, that McKiernan would ever sell your family to *you*?"

"Nothing makes me imagine that," said Peter. "But it is all I can think to do. And, Mr. Levi, if I don't do something, how can I go on?"

Levi Friedman wrote the letter. And every evening, Peter came by to see whether there was any answer from Mr. Thornton.

Finally, a letter did arrive from Friedman in Illinois.

"He said very little about Tuscumbia," Levi told Peter. "Simply that he had decided to close up the shop and move to a free state. He's traveling now, trying to decide where to settle."

"He was driven out of town," said Peter. "For helping me."

Levi protested. "Joseph left and went to California. That had nothing to do with you. Isaac decided to move—for the same reasons."

"Do you believe that, sir?" Peter asked.

Levi Friedman did not answer.

"Mr. Isaac, he loved that shop," Peter said. "He came there a peddler. He worked hard to get that shop. Him and Mr. Joseph."

"Look," said Levi Friedman, "I was wondering whether you'd want me to write a letter to Mrs. Hogun. You told me she was always kind to you. And since she's McKiernan's sister-in-law, she could tell us about your family and what's happened to them."

"Yes!" Peter exclaimed. "Miss 'Muthis! She could find out how they are!"

The two men sat together at Friedman's writing desk. They decided to send Thirmuthis Hogun a brief note signed by a Samuel Lewis: a casual note saying that a black man named Peter Gist had requested him to write said letter, inquiring as to the health and well-being of his family.

"If she thinks I took the name of Gist," said Peter, "she might remember me more kindly. She loved her first husband—my master, Levi Gist."

"So," said Friedman, "there's another Levi in your life."

Peter nodded. "But, sir, there is a big difference between the two. For a wedding present, Mr. Levi Gist gave my

183

brother three hundred and seventeen lashes with a cowhide whip."

In mid-July, "Mr. Samuel Lewis" received a response from Mrs. Thirmuthis Hogun.

She reported that the runaways had been brought back to the McKiernan plantation on Sunday, April 5. They were sent out at once to join the other slaves in planting cotton. Since every hand was needed at that crucial season, the day of vengeance had been postponed.

The following Wednesday morning, young Peter had received two hundred and fifty lashes from Smith, the overseer. Levin had received a like number of lashes. McKiernan himself had tied Vina's hands, bade her take off her coat, and gave her one hundred lashes. As for Catharine, she had escaped the cowhide altogether. "It's that devilish Peter that's been at the bottom of all this," McKiernan had said. "And I believe the Jew has done the work. Catharine didn't understand any of their plans. She's a likely wench, and it didn't seem worthwhile to whip her."

It was incredible. The punishment had been so mild!

"Neither the stocks nor the runaway's heavy irons were called into requisition," Mrs. Hogun wrote. "Why, we know not."

Peter uttered a thankful cry. But his relief was speedily tempered—by worry. Perhaps McKiernan was "saving" the victims in order to make a lesson of them when the heavy work in the cotton fields was finished.

He expressed this fear to Levi Friedman, who simply said, "You know your man McKiernan, Peter. I don't. But it is possible that he was impressed. Four slaves reaching a free state before they were found might signify money, organization, power somewhere up here in the North. He may be afraid to misuse his property."

Peter nodded, unconvinced but willing to hope.

In August another letter arrived from Mrs. Hogun, addressed to "Mr. Samuel Lewis," with news for Peter Gist. Mr. McKiernan, as was his custom, had given his slaves a barbecue when the crop was laid. This one was an especially festive affair, with pigs, chickens, sheep, and oxen roasting over the glowing coals in the long dirt trenches. The reason for the sumptuous feast: it also celebrated a wedding. Young Peter had married Susanna. McKiernan, Mrs. Hogun wrote, seemed highly pleased with the match.

Peter wondered whether his son had disobeyed him in despair, never believing that his father could fulfill the promise of bringing his family North to freedom. Perhaps he preferred life with Susanna to the fragile possibility of freedom. Or had McKiernan forced the marriage, to ensure that young Peter would remain on the plantation?

Mrs. Hogun's letter also noted that Vina had been separated from her family and sent to work on the island McKiernan owned on the river.

The news in this letter brought some relief to Peter, for at least it sounded as though McKiernan had put aside the thought of irons. He had found other ways to chain the runaways.

Several weeks later another letter arrived.

It had been mailed to William, who sent it on to Peter.

With cold and trembling fingers, Peter held the three sheets of paper, trying to make out the words. The letter was signed by B. McKiernan and was addressed to Mr. William Still. It was from South Florence, Alabama, and was dated August 6, 1851.

Some of the words and figures Peter knew: "the name of Peter Gist . . . the name of Friedman . . . Negroes . . . money . . . $1000 . . . 8000 . . . 5000 . . . 4. . . ."

But what did the letter *say?*

Peter arrived breathless at the home of Levi Friedman. He had run all the way, and his heart was thumping hard in his chest.

The serving girl showed him into the parlor. Mr. Friedman, she told him, had not yet come home. But he was due shortly.

As Peter sat waiting, he caught his breath. But his heart kept pounding. His mouth was dry. His hands still trembled. This letter, he knew, held the fate of his family. He stared at the words on the paper.

> *South Florence, Ala., 6th August, 1851*
>
> MR. WILLIAM STILL, NO. 31 NORTH FIFTH STREET, PHILADELPHIA.
>
> SIR a few days sinc mr Lewis Thornton of Tuscumbia Ala shewed me a letter dated 6 June 51 from cincinnati synd samuel Lewis in behalf of a Negro man by the name of peter Gist who informed the writer of the Letter that you were his Brother & wished an answer to be directed to you as he peter would be in Philadelphia. the object of the letter was to purchis from me 4 Negroes that is peters Wife & children 2 sons & 1 girl the Name of said Negroes are the woman viney the (mother) Eldest son peter 21 or 2 years old second son Leven 19 or 20 years 1 Girl about 13 or 14 eyars old. the Husband and Father of these people once belonged to a relation of mine by the name of Gist now Decest & some few years sinc he peter was sold to a man by the Name of Friedman who removed to Cincinnati ohio & Tuck peter with him of course peter became free by the voluntary act of the master some time last march a white man by the name of Miller apperd in the nabourhood & abducted the bove negoes was caute at vincanes Indi with said negroes & was thare convicted of steling & remanded back to Ala to Abide the penetly of the law & on his his return met his just reward by Getting drowned at the mouth of Cumberland River on the ohio

in attempting to make his escape I recovered & Braught
Back said 4 negroes or as You would say coulard people
under the Belief that peter the Husband was acsessery to
the offence thareby putting me to much Expense & Truble
to the amt $1000 which if he gets them he or his Friends
must refund these 4 negros here are worth in the market
about 4000 for tha are Extraordenary fine & likely & but
for the fact of Elopement I would not take 8000 Dollars
for them but as the thing now stands you can say to Peter
& his new discovered Relations in Philadelphi I will take
5000 for the 4 culerd people & if this will suite him & he
can raise the money I will deliver to him or his agent at
paduca at mouth of Tennessee river said negroes but the
money must be Deposited in the Hands of some respectable person at paduca before I remove the property
it wold not be safe for peter to come to this countery

write me a line on recpt of this & let me know peters
views on the above

I am Yours &c

B. McKIERNAN

NB say to peter to write & let me know his views amedi-
ately as I am determined to act in a way if he dont take
this offer he will never have an other apportunity

B. McKIERNAN


When Mr. Friedman returned and entered the parlor,
Peter stood up and handed him the letter.

Friedman's hands shook just a little as he held the three
closely written pages. When he looked up at Peter, he said,
"McKiernan is prepared to sell your wife and three children
to you for the sum of five thousand dollars."


Peter left at once for Philadelphia, hoping for help and
advice from his brother William.

The help was forthcoming. William knew of a kind and
wealthy woman in nearby Burlington, New Jersey, who was
looking for a responsible servant and carriage driver. She

would pay good wages, far more than Peter was earning in Cincinnati. And, William said, the Still family would do what they could in contributing toward the "ransom fund," as he termed it.

But William's advice contradicted the help that he offered. "It would take three lifetimes for you to save $5,000. What McKiernan asks, you can never achieve. He knows that full well."

"You're telling me to forget my family?" Peter asked.

William countered with another question. "If $5,000 fell from the heavens and you gave it to McKiernan, what guarantee do you have that the man would, as he puts it, 'deliver the four colored people'?"

Since there was no guarantee, Peter made no answer. But he did request that William write at once to Mr. McKiernan informing him that the $5,000 would be forthcoming.

Then he left for Burlington, New Jersey, where he was hired as servant and carriage driver by Mrs. Mary A. Buckman.

In addition to the higher wages, his new position had another important bonus: Mrs. Buckman and her two daughters taught Peter how to read. His first text was the New Testament. His second was a newspaper serial that William sent him. A new installment was published each week in the *National Era*, an antislavery journal. The story was called *Uncle Tom's Cabin, or The Man that Was a Thing*.

After some six months of working and saving, Peter understood the reality of William's advice. To save $5,000 in a lifetime was, for him, an impossibility. Well over a year ago he had given all his money, $54, to Seth Conklin. Since that time he had managed to save $83.

But if, as he had first hoped, he could buy Vina and his

daughter, perhaps *their* price would not be so high—possibly a total of a thousand dollars. Then, with the three of them working hard, saving, they might someday manage to ransom the two boys. As for young Peter's wife, Susanna, and the children who would certainly be coming. . . . Peter shoved that impossible problem from his mind.

First one step, and then the next.

A Dr. H. N. Ely of Medford, New Jersey, had become interested in Peter's "case," and agreed to write a letter to Lewis B. Thornton of Tuscumbia asking him to sound out McKiernan on the new approach.

Finally, at the end of August, the letter came:

*Tuscumbia, Ala., August 19th, 1852.*

H. N. ELY—Dear Sir—Your letter has remained unanswered for so long because I have not been able to have an interview with Mr. McKiernan on the subject about which you wrote. I have just seen him. He says he will not separate the family of Negroes, and the lowest price he will take under any circumstances is $5,000; and if that is placed in my hands, or with any responsible persons for him, he will let the Negroes go.

I would like Peter to get his wife and family, and think this amount a high price: but it is the lowest, I know.

Very respectfully,

LEWIS B. THORNTON.

This letter Peter could read by himself.

"Very well," he said to Dr. Ely, "the lowest price he will take for my family is $5,000. So that is what I will give him."

"Well," said the doctor, "all I can say is—good luck to you."

"I now have $100," Peter told him. "That will be the first step of the way to the $5,000."

But he had more than the $100. He had a new plan.

*189*

# 22

He had hoped that his brother William would help him.

But William flatly refused. "No abolitionist," he exclaimed, "would give you money to turn over to a slave-owner! To them it would be like handing gold to a law-breaker, a thief."

"McKiernan's not a law-breaker," said Peter. "Slavery is law in Alabama."

"According to abolitionists," said William, "slavery breaks the laws of God. And those laws are above any made by man."

"You won't help me?"

William sighed. Finally he said, "You ought not to feel so uneasy—so perfectly restless because your family are slaves. There are thousands of people as good as they who are in the same condition. Do you see that woman across the street? She is just as good as you are, and she has a mother and sister in slavery. You cannot expect people to give *you* $5,000 to buy your family, when so many others, equally deserving, are just as badly off."

"Look here," said Peter, "I know a heap of men, as good and as smart as I am, that are slaves now; but *I've bought my liberty, and my family shall be free.*"

Peter then went to Judge Boudinot, his new employer. He was happy in his job and made higher wages than ever before in his life. But he told the judge that he was leaving, and he told him why.

On a windy, snow-streaked winter day on the eighth of November, 1852, Peter Still left Burlington. He was armed with three "certificates."

*Burlington, November 6, 1852.*

Peter Still (a colored man), has lived in my employ for some months past, but I have known him for two years.

It affords me much pleasure in being able to recommend him, as an honest, sober, industrious and capable man, perfectly trustworthy and ever willing to make himself generally useful, either about the house or stable. I part with him reluctantly; he leaves me, to make an effort to redeem his wife and children from slavery.

E. E. BOUDINOT.

The above named Peter Still, was in my employ ten months, during which time he fully sustained the character given him by Mr. Boudinot. It gives me pleasure to add my name to this recommendation.

MARY A. BUCKMAN.

Judge Boudinot is one of our principal citizens, and I have entire confidence in his recommendation of Peter Still.

CORTLANDT VAN RENSSELAER.

*Burlington, N. J., Nov. 6, 1852.*

He also had a letter of introduction from a Mr. McKim of Philadelphia to a Rev. Mr. May of Syracuse, New York. The Rev. Mr. May was, according to Mr. McKim, a great lover of humanity who would certainly be of help to Peter in his cause.

And the Rev. Mr. May did, indeed, listen to Peter with the greatest sympathy. *He* gave Peter a letter of introduction to a Rev. Mr. Millard in Auburn, New York.

The Rev. Mr. Millard read Peter's growing collection of letters and asked, "What exactly would you like me to do?"

"I—I thought, sir," Peter said, his words stumbling, "if I could speak to a group of people—not abolitionists, just good people—if I could tell them about my Vina, my daughter Catharine, my sons—" He broke off.

"Yes?" the Rev. Mr. Millard said. His voice was kind, encouraging.

"Might be," said Peter swiftly, "they would help me by giving money."

Mr. Millard pursed his lips and frowned. Finally he said, "There are, I have read, over two million slaves in the South. What makes your family special?"

"They're special—to me," Peter said softly.

Presently the Rev. Mr. Millard said, "Have you ever *asked* any group of people to help you in raising this $5,000?"

Peter shook his head. "Just my brothers and sisters up here in the North."

"And will they help?"

"As best they can. Fifty or a hundred dollars. And my brother John gave me this suit that I'm wearing."

The Rev. Mr. Millard sighed. Then he said, "Come to my church tonight. I'll bring you up to the pulpit and introduce you. You tell your story to the people and ask for help. We'll see what happens. But don't be disappointed if you're met with silence—and no contributions at all."

"Yes, sir, Reverend," Peter said fervently. "Thank you, sir."

"Don't thank me yet, Peter. Nothing may come of it."

That evening after the sermon, the Rev. Mr. Millard brought Peter up to the pulpit and informed the congregation that their visitor, Peter Still, had a message they might want to hear.

Then Mr. Millard stepped back.

Peter looked out at the audience. Not only was he too terrified to utter a word, but he had to lean on the pulpit to keep from falling. The bones in his legs seemed to turn to water. He stared at the people. They stared back at him.

Then several stood up and started to leave. Others snickered.

The Rev. Mr. Millard came forward, and it was he who told Peter's story. When he had finished he turned to Peter, who had stopped trembling and was now able to utter a few sentences. "As you see," he told the white faces spaced out there in the evening gloom, "I'm mighty scared. But when I put my thoughts onto my wife, my daughter, my boys . . . then I can find the words I come here to say to you. I need your help to buy my family. To buy their freedom."

A collection plate was passed. The coins added up to $3.05. But a few of the churchgoers came over to talk to Peter. He was invited to speak at a school, at a factory, and at a home.

In these less formal settings he found words. He was able to tell his story without aid. When he left Auburn a week later, he had $50 to add to his fund. He also had a letter of introduction to a clergyman in Rochester. Before traveling to that city he stopped briefly in Waterloo, where he got some assistance. In Rochester he spoke at two churches, a men's club, and at the homes of several leading citizens. When he left Rochester, his fund had grown to $200.

In order to use all his time fruitfully, he took to ringing the doorbells of strangers while he waited for the evening hour when he was scheduled to speak.

The first time he knocked, the master of the house answered the door. When he had heard Peter's first few sentences, he cursed him loudly and cried out, "It's all a damned lie! You ought to be arrested! There's a lazy pack of you that make it a business to go around whining about having families in slavery. It's time it was stopped!" He slammed the front door.

Peter walked quietly down the street and presently knocked at another door. This time a middle-aged matron answered and invited him inside. When she had looked at his letters and heard his story, she informed him serenely that slaves were far better off than free Negroes. "Indeed," she said, "I know all about it, for my mother owns plenty of them, and not one of her slaves is obliged to work so hard as I do myself. Here the free Negroes are begging around, many of them half-starved, and some of them are stealing and going to prison."

"Yes, ma'am," Peter answered politely. "They do that, both white and colored. It is not the colored people alone that beg and steal. And I have been told that there are more white people in prison than black ones."

"Well, that may be. But," she concluded, "the Negroes are better off in the South, where they are all taken good care of."

Peter wondered whether *she* would like to be a happy, well-fed slave herself. But he refrained from asking the question; instead he thanked her for her time and left.

After a few more encounters of this sort, he decided that the only way to proceed on his quest was the way in which he had started: with letters directing him to white men who were already known to be sympathetic to the antislavery cause.

To white men—and to white women; one woman, in any case.

The newspaper series he had so painstakingly read had now been published as a book. Peter saw it everywhere, in shops and in homes. People sat reading it on trains, in horse-drawn carriages, and stagecoaches; they read it in railroad station waiting rooms, restaurants, barber shops. And the woman who wrote the book had herself become a heroine. If he could obtain a letter from Harriet Beecher Stowe!

He learned that she was the daughter of one clergyman, the wife of another, and the sister of seven more. Surely a woman with so much God and goodness in her family and in her writing would listen to his story and would help him.

He also learned that she lived near Boston.

Snow was sifting from the sky on the day Peter arrived in Boston. It was late December, near Christmas, and the views that spread before him as he walked the streets were like a living series of the Christmas cards he had seen displayed in shops and homes during the past few weeks.

Sleighs and delivery pungs gliding over hard-packed snow, with children in bright winter clothing, clinging to the rear and standing on the runners. . . . Gentlemen in black broadcloth coats and fur caps driving two-wheeled, one-horse carriages. . . . Ladies tucked snugly in fur robes, out for a drive in a stylish gig. . . . A coachman in a tall hat and caped greatcoat, sitting high in his Hansom cab waiting for a customer, taking a "nip" now and then from a pottery bottle cast in the shape of his own figure replete with top hat and coat. . . . And jingling sleighbells resounding through the sunny blue morning.

He stopped several people to ask the way to the Anti-Slavery Office. Each time he did so he was greeted with courtesy and kindness. One man accompanied him for two blocks to point out the way.

As he walked through the streets of Boston, Peter became convinced that he would receive help in this beautiful city. He passed by row upon row of elegant townhouses built of brick and brownstone; each had a high front stoop, decorative iron railings, and a small lawn covered with snow sparkling in the sunlight. As for the shops, they were the most splendid he had ever seen. He dreamed of the time when he might bring his wife to this city. Vina had never even heard of snow.

The young man at the Anti-Slavery Office not only knew the address of Harriet Beecher Stowe, but he knew the author herself. She had come often to this very office when she was gathering material for *Uncle Tom's Cabin*. "Some of the characters and incidents," the young man said, "are based on true case histories which Mrs. Stowe read sitting at the very table where you are sitting now."

Having learned the value of introduction letters, Peter now requested one addressed to Mrs. Stowe. The young man, who had heard of Peter's brother William Still in the Philadelphia Anti-Slavery Office, willingly gave Peter the letter. But, like Peter's brother, he expressed disapproval of Peter's plan. Futhermore, he was certain that Mrs. Stowe would refuse her help. No abolitionist would give money to enrich a slave-owner. It was against every principle the abolitionists stood for.

"With those principles," Peter said, "I would still be a slave."

He took the stagecoach to Andover, Massachusetts, where Mrs. Stowe lived.

Darkness had settled over the town by the time he reached it, and with nightfall came a chill, cutting wind.

He found the street and the house, but stood for a while on the doorstep shivering, afraid to lift the knocker.

Finally he did so.

The door was opened by a small, middle-aged woman with dark hair drawn straight back. "Yes?" she inquired.

"Please, ma'am," said Peter. "Would you give this letter to Mrs. Stowe?"

She took the letter, said, "Just a moment, please," and shut the door, leaving Peter out in the windy darkness.

A few moments later she reopened the door and said, "I'm Mrs. Stowe. Come in, please. May I take your coat?"

As she led him into the parlor, she said, "You must forgive me for not inviting you in at once. So many people come here to meet me, to ask for favors. I should have no life at all if I let everyone in."

She motioned Peter to a seat by the bright, crackling fire in the hearth. "Now," she said, "tell me why *you* have come."

He started by saying that *Uncle Tom's Cabin* was the first book he had ever read.

She nodded and said nothing. And he realized she must have heard this statement many times, so he launched at once into his story. When he had finished, he took out the newspaper clipping that recounted how Conklin had died. Mrs. Stowe read it and exclaimed, "They killed him, of course. Threw him overboard. They knew he couldn't swim, shackled as he was!"

"No," said Peter, "I believe that he did try to escape, like it says in the paper. He was a man who treasured freedom. For everyone. I think Seth Conklin would risk drowning, rather than spend his years in an Alabama jail cell. He took the risk, and he lost."

"A man who should be long remembered," said Mrs. Stowe.

"He gave his life to try to save my family," Peter said softly. "Now that he is gone, I am trying to do that myself —in the best way that I know." He told her then of his plan. And he took out the letters about himself that he had gathered along the way.

As she read through them he sat stiffly. If this woman agreed to help him, he was certain that he would succeed.

He gazed at the table before him. It was covered by a long, fringed cloth, and piled high with books and albums. There were also a rose jar of dried petals and a humidor for cigars.

He willed the words that he wanted her to say.

And presently she said them. "All right. I will help you."

She went to the desk by the window and sat writing. The dark velvet drapes that framed the tall window behind her made a backdrop for a picture he knew he would never forget.

She wrote for several minutes. Then she turned to him and said, "Do you think this will help you?" And she read:

"Having examined the claims of this unfortunate man, I am satisfied that his is a case that calls for compassion and aid.

"Though the sum demanded is so large as to look hopeless, yet if every man who is so happy as to be free, and have his own wife and children *for his own*, would give even a small amount, the sum might soon be raised.

"As ye would that men should do for you—do ye even so for them—H. B. Stowe."

# 23

---◆---

With this letter from Harriet Beecher Stowe, the question became not whether Peter could raise the $5,000, but how soon he could do so.

He was told that it would take a decade to raise such an impossible sum. Meanwhile, Vina would be nearing sixty; McKiernan would have worked her dry, and she would be of no use to the slave-owner or to herself. McKiernan would have had the best working years from young Peter and Levin. And who knew how many children his boy Peter would have fathered during that time? Would they too have to be ransomed? And Peter's wife, Susanna?

There was only one answer to all the questions: *Hurry.* Forget sleep. Forget comfort. Speak to whoever would listen. Save. Get the bank account growing. Get more letters. More contacts. Move on. *Hurry!*

Two weeks after he met Mrs. Stowe, this notice appeared in a Boston newspaper:

*Boston, January 3, 1853.*
The bearer, Peter Still, was kidnapped in early childhood, on the borders of Delaware river, in New Jersey, and carried thence to Kentucky, and subsequently to Alabama. After being held in slavery more than forty years, he succeeded in purchasing his freedom; and being obliged, consequently, by the laws of Alabama, to leave that State,

he came North to Philadelphia, where, by a strange coincidence, he became acquainted with his brother and family, from which he had been so long severed. He has left a wife and three children in Alabama, whom he naturally and ardently desires to bring into freedom, and have with him at the North. For this purpose he now appeals to the sympathy of the benevolent for such pecuniary aid as they may be disposed to give him.

We, the undersigned, have carefully examined his letters and papers, and have obtained knowledge of him. From this examination, we are satisfied that his story is true in all its particulars; that he is himself a worthy and virtuous man, whose extraordinary history gives him a strong and peculiar claim upon the public sympathy and aid.

Any contributions for the object above named may be forwarded to any of us.

S. K. LOTHROP,
ELLIS GRAY LORING,
EPHRAIM PEABODY,
WM. J. BOWDITCH,
J. I. BOWDITCH,
JOHN P. ROBINSON,
THOS. STARR KING.

The notice also appeared in newspapers of neighboring towns that Peter visited. He remained in Boston and the vicinity until the end of March, at which time he was able to deposit $460 in what he termed his Freedom Account.

He then took the train north to Portland, Maine, where he had a letter of introduction addressed to the Hon. Neal Dow. He left that city one week later—with $100.

The weeks and months that followed became for Peter a hectic kaleidoscope. He seemed to be constantly riding trains. The railroad cars were rattling containers of the winter cold. Most carriages had a wood-burning stove at each end. Peter soon learned that to sit by the stove meant slowly roasting, and choking on the foul air. He found it preferable to select a seat in the middle and slowly freeze.

When springtime came, traveling by train was somewhat more comfortable. Windows were opened. At the start of such a journey he was often the only black passenger aboard. By the end of the trip, all were black from the engine soot that flew in.

Often, when he reached his destination, Peter could scarcely walk. His back pained him badly from the constant, jolting ride on the narrow, straight-backed wooden seat.

The carriage floors were slippery with tobacco juice and rotted scraps of food. At every stop, hawkers selling fruit and cake rushed through each car. Sometimes a boy came aboard with a tin watering pot in one hand and a few greasy drinking glasses in the other. There were many days when these items were Peter's sole food and drink.

In addition to discomfort, the railroads could often mean danger. On occasion, steam engines blew up. Cows or hogs straying onto the tracks caused accidents. And some tracks were so badly laid that the flat bar-rail would spring, the spikes would not hold, and the end of the rail with its sharp point would rip through the floor of the passing car. The passengers called this a "snake's head." And the unlucky traveler who chanced to be sitting over the snake's head was likely to be spitted like a roasting pig and impaled against the roof.

But in contrast, when Peter arrived at each new destination, he was often treated like an honored guest. He rarely spent money at hotels or inns. Sometimes he slept in the home of a black family in town. But frequently he would find himself the sole occupant of a luxurious guest room with an imported cut-glass chandelier, a soft carpet, watered-silk upholstery, and a high canopied bed.

By the end of May he had visited Brunswick, Bath, Saco, Biddeford, Portsmouth, Hampton, Newburyport, and Garretson Station. And he had collected $490.

In towns in New Jersey he collected a total of $75. In Syracuse, New York, he raised $120. By the end of July he found himself in Peterboro, with a letter of introduction to the wealthy abolitionist Gerrit Smith. He was invited to spend the night in Smith's simple cottage. And he departed the next morning with a generous sum for his Freedom Account, plus the following note:

I am, and have long been deeply interested in the case of the bearer, Peter Still. I hope he may meet with generous friends wherever he shall go.

GERRIT SMITH

*Peterboro, July 27, 1853.*

New Bedford: $115. . . . Lowell: $185. . . . Somerville: $36. . . . Cambridge: $19. . . .

In Worcester, Massachusetts, he was aided by a notice placed in the *Worcester Spy* by the famous writer Edward E. Hale, author of *Man Without a Country*.

*Worcester, September 8, 1853*

We would take this method of commending to the attention of all Christians and friends of humanity, the bearer, Peter Still. We heard his story, and examined his letters of introduction when he first came to Boston, in December last, and are satisfied of his worthiness to be encouraged and helped as he needs. He has been welcomed to many hearts in New England, and he will be to many more. All ye who can, give him aid and comfort.

J. G. ADAMS
A. HILL
EDWARD E. HALE.

He spent two weeks in Worcester and came away with $150.

Then, back on the hot, rattling train, to Plymouth . . . Kingston . . . and Fall River, where he met the noted abolitionist Asa Bronson, who sent him on his way with a letter addressed to the citizens of Providence, Rhode Island:

To the disciples of Christ and the friends of humanity in Providence, R.I.:

I have carefully examined the various letters and documents of Peter Still; and I fully believe that he is entitled to the entire confidence, cordial sympathy, and generous aid of the Christian public. We have assisted him in Fall River and vicinity to the amount of about $200.

Help him if you can. "He that hath pity on the poor, lendeth to the Lord."

> With due respect,
> Yours,
> ASA BRONSON

Peter spent November in Providence and left with $250 received from 140 separate individuals. On, then, to Roxbury . . . Charleston . . . back to Woburn and Cambridge. . . . And finally, in the first month of the new year, to New York City. There, in a single month, he raised a staggering sum: $1,146.45. He also obtained a letter, addressed to the editor of the Albany *Evening Journal*, from one of the most important men in America—the editor in chief of the New York *Tribune*:

MY OLD FRIEND: Peter Still, who will hand you this, was . . . kidnapped when six years old, with his brother, two years older, and sold into slavery; served forty years in Alabama; finally bought himself free, leaving his wife and three children in the hands of the scoundrels who had robbed him of forty years' work; and he is now begging money to buy them out of bondage. His chivalrous robber only asks him $5,000 for his own wife and children. It is robbery to pay it, but inhumanity to refuse; and, as the time has not yet arrived for paying such villains with lead and steel, rather than gold, I wish you could help him to raise a part of the money among those you know.

Yours,

HORACE GREELEY

GEORGE DAWSON, ESQ.

ALBANY EVENING JOURNAL OFFICE.


In Albany Peter collected $75. On, then, to Pittsfield, Massachusetts: $105. Thence to Springfield: $100. And to New Haven, Connecticut, where he remained for a month and collected $300 by speaking before 250 different groups. These included "Carpenter's Millinery Help," "Ladies in Shirt Factory," "Workmen in Clock Factory," "Young Ladies of Miss Dutton's School," "Lancasterian School," "Ladies of the Rubber Factory," and "Pupils of Webster High School."

He went on and on, through the steaming hot summer months of 1854. Hartford: $300. . . . Wethersfield: $21. . . . Middletown: $126. . . . Meriden: $80. . . . Bridgeport: $126. . . . New London: $115. . . . Norwich: $100. . . . Northampton: $45. . . . Buffalo: $80. . . . He ventured as far north as Toronto, Canada: $15. . . And he went to the little village of Camillus, New York, which had but two churches. He spoke at both of them. The Rev. Mr. Bush of the Methodist Church introduced Peter Still by saying: "He can succeed without our aid. *But we cannot afford to miss this opportunity!*" The Camillus churchgoers contributed $63 to the Freedom Account.


Finally, in early December 1854, Peter Still returned to Philadelphia. He was thin, ill, and near collapse from exhaustion. It had taken him two years. He had visited some towns and cities four and five times. But he had collected the $5,000.

McKiernan had specified in his letter that "the money must be Deposited in the Hands of some respectable person at paduca before I remove the property." And he had thoughtfully noted that "it wold not be safe for peter to come to this countery."

Consequently, Peter made arrangements with a wealthy merchant, a Mr. Hollowell of Philadelphia, who in turn opened negotiations with a Mr. John Simpson of Florence, Alabama. As soon as the funds were brought to him, Mr. Simpson would go to McKiernan and buy Peter's family.

A clerk of the House of Hollowell & Co. was sent to Florence, Alabama, carrying two pistols and Peter's $5,000. He was instructed to give the money to John Simpson. And then escort Peter's family to Cincinnati.

Early Saturday morning, on the last day of 1854, Peter Still and Levi Friedman stood by the wharf, waiting for the *Northerner* to arrive at Cincinnati. The Hollowell clerk had sent a telegram from Louisville giving the name of the boat and the probable time of arrival.

A cold wind, streaked with sleet, swept in from the river. The sky was hung with heavy clouds.

Peter turned up his coat collar and said, "I wish the sun was shining for them."

"They'll have all the sun they'll want to see," Levi told him, "when they look at your face."

Peter smiled. Then he said, "I'm glad you're here with me, Mr. Levi. Seems right, somehow. Without your brothers, Mr. Joseph and Mr. Isaac, I'd never be standing here a free man, waiting for my family."

"You have only one person to thank for that," said Levi.

Peter looked at him.

"Yourself," said Levi. "I've never heard of anyone who's ever done what you have done in the past year. You, Peter Still, have made your own little piece of history."

Peter laughed. Then he blew on his fingers, which felt like ten icicles. "I'm not worried much about history. I'm worried that we might freeze solid before the boat ever gets here."

"Would you like to go up to a coffee house?" Levi asked. "We can still see the packet when she comes round the bend."

"No, sir," Peter said. "Seems like I'd rather be right here in place, ready to run up that gangplank soon as that old boat pulls in. But you go, sir. Go in someplace and warm yourself."

"Seems like I'd rather be right here, too," Levi said. Then he asked, "What are your plans, Peter? After you leave Cincinnati?"

"First we're going to see my old mother," Peter said. "When I left she was quoting the Bible at me: 'I had not thought to see thy face, and lo, God hath showed me also thy seed.' Israel said that," he added, "to Joseph in the Bible."

"Yes," said Levi Friedman, "I know."

"Jews read the Bible?" said Peter.

"The Old Testament," said Levi. "In fact, Jews wrote it."

Peter looked at him in some surprise. Then he said, "After we visit my mother and the rest of my family, Catharine will stay with my brother William in Philadelphia. And she will go to school." The words sounded so remarkable that he repeated them slowly, "She will go to school." His daughter, Catharine, a sixteen-year-old slave girl who could not count to ten or write her name—Catharine would be starting school.

"Mr. Richard Ely in New Hope, Pennsylvania, has offered a job to my boy Peter, as house servant and carriage driver. And Levin will be a blacksmith's apprentice in Beverly, New Jersey."

"And your wife?"

"Vina and I will be together. Working together for the first time. We will work at a big boardinghouse in Burlington, New Jersey. And then, the way I plan it, we will buy us our own house."

Levi pointed suddenly and said, "Is that a steamboat coming?"

Far down at the bend of the river, a dark shape showed in the dense mist. It could have been any river boat—a coal barge, a ferry, a flatboat. But Peter knew it was the *Northerner*.

The boat moved closer, a passenger boat. He could hear the bright music of the calliope. Then the mist lifted; two American flags waved in the winter wind, and black-painted letters were clear by the paddlewheel: NORTHERNER.

"My God, Mr. Levi," Peter whispered. "I'm so scared they won't be on board."

The quay was suddenly crowded with shouting, shoving people; some had come to meet passengers, some to collect freight. And the three decks of the steamboat were crowded with men and women waving. Some shouted greetings to those on shore.

"I can't see them," Peter cried. "Mr. Levi, I can't see my family nowhere!"

"Maybe they're below," Levi Friedman said. "To get out of the cold."

The two men were among the first to go aboard. Peter

pushed here, there—shoving, searching. He lost Levi Friedman. He couldn't find his family. "Please," he kept saying to anyone who would listen to him. "I'm looking for my family. My wife. My daughter. My two boys."

"Sorry," a few said. Most did not answer but shook free from his clutching hand and hurried on. One man cursed him and said, "Get out of my way, damned crazy nigger."

And then Peter saw his wife in the doorway. She was clutching a black shawl close about her.

*"Vina!"*

She saw him. They ran to each other. He folded his arms tight around her. "Oh, my God," he kept saying. "Oh, my God, you are here."

His eyes were wet, but he could make out the blurry shape of his daughter Catharine in the doorway. Then his sons came up from below.

"I'll be dead from the cold," Vina said, laughing, crying, shivering. "Before I set foot on free soil, I'll be dead from the cold."

Levi Friedman found them then. "Look," he said, "you wait inside. I'll get a carriage. Then we'll all go to my house. We've got a good hot breakfast waiting."

An hour later they sat in Levi Friedman's dining room. A fire in the hearth spread warmth and welcome. Peter laughed at the open astonishment on his wife's face when she was served breakfast by the white girl named Kathleen.

His sons and his daughter ate a good deal and said very little.

Finally, Peter asked the question that had been pressing on his mind for months. He turned to his oldest son. "Your wife, Susanna?"

"Susanna," said young Peter, "is dead."

"Dead?" Peter whispered.

His son nodded. "We had us two children. Little Edmund was four months old when he died. Then the second baby was born. We called him Peter. After his granddaddy. But the overseer sent Susanna out to work too soon. Sent her out to the fields in a heavy rain. She took sick. One Sunday morning she said to me, 'You take good care of our little baby.' And then she died."

"And where is that baby? My grandson Peter?"

"McKiernan says he will sell him to me for $200. I figgered he would let me take my baby North. But at the last minute, that is what he said to me. Two hundred dollars. Where we going to get $200? So we had to go off and leave my baby crying there. I can hear him crying right now, inside my head."

"Look, son," said Peter, "if I can raise $5,000, won't take me no trouble to raise $200 more."

"We can no doubt do that tomorrow night," said Levi Friedman. He glanced at Peter. "I should have told you this before, perhaps, but—" he hesitated. "I'm a trustee of the Temple B'nai Jeshurun here in Cincinnati. We planned a sort of—celebration. To raise money. We want to be sure that your family has a proper sendoff, for the new year. And for your new life—together. It seems to me, a new baby is a most suitable New Year's gift." He shoved his chair back from the table. "If you'll excuse me, I think I'll hunt up that clerk from Hollowell. He might just be taking another trip back to South Florence before he heads home to Philadelphia."

And Levi Friedman hurried from the room.

When he had gone, young Peter said softly, "Susanna told me, 'take care of our baby.' Maybe that little boy will grow up without ever knowing he was born a slave."

Peter looked around the table. His wife sat beside him. He took her hand. His daughter, Catharine, sat across from him. Next month she would be starting school. His two sons were watching him. The younger boy looked very like his dead brother, Levin.

A family, together around a breakfast table. A simple matter. An ordinary scene. Foolish to call it a miracle.

# Bibliography

As stated in the Author's Note, this book is a retelling of Peter Still's story as he narrated it in Kate E. R. Pickard's *The Kidnapped and the Redeemed* (Syracuse, N.Y.: W. T. Hamilton, 1856. Reprinted 1941 by the Negro Publication Society of America under the title *The Kidnapped and the Ransomed*). Two of Peter's brothers also wrote books. These, and material about William Still, were used in the supplementary research concerning the family and the era.

Gara, Larry. "William Still." *Pennsylvania History Journal*, vol. 28, no. 1 (1961), pp. 33–44. Philadelphia: Pennsylvania Historical Association.

Still, Dr. James. *Early Recollections and Life of Dr. James Still, 1812–1885*. Medford, N.J.: Medford Historical Society, 1971.

Still, William. *The Underground Railroad*. Philadelphia: Porter and Coates, 1872.

The following books were used for additional background information about the period.

*American Jewish Archives*, Vol. IX. Cincinnati: Hebrew Union College Press, 1957.

Andrews, Edward D. *The People Called Shakers*. New York: Oxford University Press, 1953.

Armitage, Merle. *Railroads of America*. Boston: Duell, Sloane, 1952.

Bancroft, Frederic. *Slave Trading in the Old South*. New York: Frederick Ungar, 1931.

Boorstin, Daniel. *The Americans*. New York: Random House, 1965.

Brewer, Fredrika. *Homes of the New World*. New York: Harper's, 1853.

Chambers, William. *Things As They Are in America*. Philadelphia: Lippincott, Grambo & Co., 1854.

Coffin, Levi. "Friends, Ancient and Modern." Pamphlet. Cincinnati, 1915.

————. *Reminiscences*. New York: A. M. Kelley, 1968. Reprint of 1876 edition.

Coles, Arthur Charles. *The Irrepressible Conflict, 1850–1865*. New York: Macmillan, 1934.

Colton, Calvin. *The Life and Times of Henry Clay*. New York: A. S. Barnes & Co., 1846.

Crabb, A. L. *Home to Kentucky*. Indianapolis: Bobbs-Merrill, 1953.

Davidson, Marshall B. *Life in America*. Boston: Houghton Mifflin, 1951.

Denison, John H. *Emotional Currents in American History*. New York: Scribner's, 1932.

Diamond, Augustus. *Levi Coffin*. London: Headley Bros., 1915.

Dinnerstein, Leonard, and Palsson, Mary Dale, eds. *Jews in the South*. Baton Rouge: Louisiana State University Press, 1973.

Dunbar, Seymour. *The History of Travel in America*. Indianapolis: Bobbs-Merrill, 1915.

Dunlop, Richard. *Doctors of the American Frontier*. Garden City, N.Y.: Doubleday, 1965.

Flexner, James T. *Doctors on Horseback*. New York: Viking, 1937.

Fogel, Robert M., and Engerman, Stanley L. *Time on the Cross*. Boston: Little, Brown, 1974.

Foner, Philip S. *The Jews in American History, 1654–1865*. New York: International Publishers, 1964.

Genovese, Eugene D. *The Political Economy of Slavery*. New York: Random House, Pantheon Books, 1965.

Handlin, Oscar. *The Americans*. Boston: Little, Brown, 1963.

Harrington, J. C. "Seventeenth Century Brickmaking." *Virginia Magazine of History and Biography*, vol. 58 (1950).

Heller, James G. *As Yesterday When It Is Past, 1842–1942*. Cincinnati: privately printed by Isaac M. Wise Temple, 1942.

Hesseltine, William B. *The South in American History*. New York: Prentice-Hall, 1943.

Holborn, Hajo. *A History of Modern Germany*, Vol. III. New York: Knopf, 1964.

Hungerford, Edward. *Story of the Baltimore and Ohio Railroad, 1827–1927*. New York: Putnam's, 1928.

Johnston, Johanna. *Runaway to Heaven*. Garden City, N.Y.: Doubleday, 1963.

Kemble, Frances Anne. *Journal of a Residence on a Georgian Plantation in 1838–1839*. Edited and with an introduction by John A. Scott. New York: Knopf, 1961.

Korn, Bertram W. *Jews and Negro Slavery in the Old South, 1789–1865*. Publication of the American Jewish Historical Society. Philadelphia: March 1961.

Lester, Julius. *To Be a Slave*. New York: Dial Press, 1968.

Lincoln, C. Eric. *The Negro Pilgrimage in America*. New York: Bantam, 1967.

Loggins, Vernon. *The Negro Author*. Port Washington, N.Y.: Kennikat Press, 1931.

Lyell, Charles. *Travels in North America, 1841–1842*. London: John Murray, 1845.

Mallory, Daniel, ed. *Henry Clay*. New York: Van Amringe and Bixby, 1844.

Marcus, J. R. *American Jewry: Documents*, American Jewish Archives Publication No. 3. Cincinnati: Hebrew Union College Press, 1959.

Mayo, Bernard. *Henry Clay*. Boston: Houghton Mifflin, 1937.

McBride, Henry Alexander. *Trains Rolling*. New York: Macmillan, 1953.

*Occident, The*. German language weekly. Philadelphia: published 1843–1868.

Parsons, C. G., M.D. *Inside View of Slavery*. Boston: J. P. Jewett & Co., 1855, and Cleveland: O. Jewett, Proctor and Worthington, 1855.

Phillips, Ulrich. *Life and Labor in the Old South*. Boston: Little, Brown, 1929.

"Plantation Diary from 1844–1852." *Louisiana Historical Quarterly*, vols. 33, 34, October 1950.

Rogers, Joseph M. *The True Henry Clay*. Philadelphia: J. B. Lippincott, 1904.

Rossiter, William S., ed. *Days and Ways in Old Boston*. Boston: R. H. Stearns & Co., 1915.

Scott, John A. *Ballad of America*. New York: Bantam, 1966.

Sellers, James B. *Slavery in Alabama*. University, Ala.: University of Alabama Press, 1950.

Smith, Richard R. *Alabama, A Guide to the Deep South*. New York: Alabama Federal Writers Project, Alabama State Planning Commission, 1941.

Stokes Collection. Early Views of New York City. New York Public Library.

Stowe, Charles E., and Beecher, Lyman. *Harriet Beecher Stowe*. Boston: Houghton Mifflin, 1911.

Van Deusen, Glyndon G. *The Life of Henry Clay*. Boston: Little, Brown, 1937.

Wagenknecht, E. C. *Harriet Beecher Stowe*. New York: Oxford University Press, 1965.

Ward, Elizabeth Stuart. *Chapters from a Life*. Cambridge: Riverside Press, 1896.

Ward, James A. "History of the Pennsylvania Railroad." *Journal of the Pennsylvania Historical Society*, January 1971.

Warner, I. W. "The Immigrants' Guide and Citizens' Manual." Pamphlet. New York, 1848.

Wilcox, R. Turner. *Five Centuries of American Costume*. New York: Scribner's, 1963.

Wilson, R. Forrest. *Crusader in Crinoline: The Life of Harriet Beecher Stowe*. Philadelphia: J. B. Lippincott, 1941.

Bills of Sale, Certificate of Freedom, and letters appeared in both editions of Kate E. R. Pickard's book.